# Visiting Emily

# Visiting Emily

Poems Inspired by
the Life & Work of
Emily Dickinson
Edited by Sheila Coghill
& Thom Tammaro

Foreword by Robert Bly

University of Iowa Press

Iowa City

University of Iowa Press, Iowa City 52242
Printed in the United States of America
Design by Richard Hendel
Illustration used on pages i, iii, and xxi by
Barry Moser
http://www.uiowa.edu/~uipress

The publication of this book was generously
supported by the University of Iowa Foundation.

Printed on acid-free paper

Library of Congress
Cataloging-in-Publication Data
Visiting Emily: poems inspired by the life
and work of Emily Dickinson / edited by
Sheila Coghill and Thom Tammaro.
        p.      cm.
Includes index.
ISBN 0-87745-734-4 (cloth), ISBN 0-87745-739-5
(pbk.)
        1. Dickinson, Emily, 1830–1886–Poetry.
2. American poetry–20th century.    I. Coghill,
Sheila, 1952–.    II. Tammaro, Thom.

PS595.D5V57    2000
811'.4–dc21                        00-034393

00    01    02    03    04    C    5    4    3    2    1
      01    02    03    04    P    5    4    3    2

EMILY

*In Amherst when someone leans out of a car window*
*and asks the way to Emily's grave, one does not ask, "Emily who?"*
— *Robert Francis*

# Contents

Avid readers of contemporary poetry, as well as teachers and devotees of Dickinson's poetry, we discovered, over the years, in poetry magazines as well as in collections of poems by individual writers, a number of poems that seemed to be inspired by the life and work of Dickinson. Because of our teacherly habits, we began photocopying and collecting these poems. Eventually we found our file folder bulging. The folder of poems presented us with the obvious question: why Dickinson – why does she, among hundreds of American poets, evoke such a response?

Perhaps of all American poets, Dickinson's popularity among general readers supersedes that of others. Ask anyone on the street to name an American poet and surely Dickinson will be one of them (Frost and Whitman probably will be among them, too). One reason for this might be that few, if any, American poets are encountered at all levels of our education – in elementary school, in junior and senior high school, in college, in graduate school. Who can forget first reading "I'm Nobody? Who are You?" sometime in elementary school?

And perhaps Dickinson remains imprinted in our minds because of that single, haunting daguerreotype that we have lived with all our lives – the one we have seen repeatedly in books, magazines, on posters and postcards, the one that flashes in our minds when her name is spoken. Unlike other American poets, whose multiple images and portraits from the various stages of their lives we carry in our memory (again, think of the many youthful *and* late adulthood images we have of Frost and Whitman), we have but one haunting image of Dickinson, made sometime in 1847 or 1848, gazing back at us through time and space. Unlike Frost or Whitman, we have not heard Dickinson's recorded voice.

When we started this project, we looked for poems inspired by the life and work of Dickinson. Little did we know it would have the corresponding riveting effect of her epistolary invitation to her brother Austin: "into my garden come" [letter, 1851]; it did not take long to gather enough material for two anthologies. So persistently unknowable to the material mind, yet so persistently evocative to the imaginations of writers, academics, and lay people alike, Dickinson's *katabasis* – the Greek term for the seamless transition from one state of consciousness to another – offers us the enticing immediacy of her poetic garden; it is an irresistible invitation to step from this realm into another. The intellectual range and thematic focus, the unbounded center of her images simultaneously haunt and elude us. Of course this makes her American muse *par excellence*, as we believe the following collection of poems illustrates.

To those who have had the opportunity to make the pilgrimage to Amherst, the Dickinson plot in the cemetery, the Dickinson homestead on Main Street, and Dickinson's bedroom, those tangible objects inspire a wealth of reflective and meditative opportunities. In fact, in some ironic way (one we think Dickinson would enjoy), the pilgrim visiting Dickinson and Amherst is immediately challenged *not* to respond! But who among us can resist the urge to speak with her, to connect with her and her world, to find words for our own intuitive and emotive responses to her life and work?

Sharon Olds sees "Emily Dickinson's Writing Table" and "the chair next to her writing table / is the chair my parents tied me to / that day. Not the same chair / but a cousin of it." Or Barry Goldensohn sees her looking "Down through the cross of her windows / facing the West [to see] / her father" or "children crouch on the lawn," farmers riding "their wagons that screech under flax and corn" and "mostly the garden change / from crocus to tulip to rose." Visiting her grave with Robert Francis, Robert Bly sees the austere "black iron fence . . . its ovals delicate as wine stems" and her being put to rest "one day . . . carried over the lots between by six Irish laboring men, when her brother refused to trust her body to a carriage. The coffin . . . darkened by violets and pine boughs, as she covered the immense distance between the solid Dickinson house and this plot. . . ."

Dickinson equally inspires writers to imagine the act of writing itself, imagining her at work, writing her poems as they themselves then write poems about her, or imagining her encountering others puzzling over her poetry. The Irish poet Michael Longley thinks of her "Wakening early each morning to write, / Dressing with care for the act of poetry." Or Theodore Weiss articulates her inscrutability: "But you will never give them / what they want and so they want / it more." And one Vermont summer Dave Etter "Walking this morning through the forest, / cool and damp and sweet . . . [finds] the skin of a birch tree" and thinks "of you now, Emily, – / knowing that you in your sure-footed joy / would know what secrets are revealed here."

And secrets multiply in Emily Dickinson, for all that we can know about her and her poetry has the bittersweet counterbalance of what we can never know. She is tangible, unruly, ineffable; she is her own riddle. Tom Koontz captures her momentary essence: "We hear her in the distance / at odd hours, qualifying notes, repealing chords."

Inspiring or maddening, frustrating or catalyzing, whimsically or calculatingly eccentric? We cannot know, except to know she deliberately taunts us with not knowing how to entertain herself. Inevitably then, Dickinson's wit, her playfulness, makes itself known. In Andrea Carlisle's "Emily Dickinson's To-Do List" who cannot see her pondering at the beginning of her week: "Monday, Figure out what to wear — white dress?" Then, proceeding through the week to "Write poem / Hide poem" or "Eavesdrop on visitors from behind door" to "Gardening — watch out for narrow fellows in grass!" And imagine Emily Dickinson in your own writing workshop as Jayne Relaford Brown has, and having to be the teacher who must offer constructive comments on "My life had stood — a Loaded Gun —." Where would you start? Do you recommend the poem needs a title? Do you ask pointed questions such as: why all the capitals? why all the dashes? Do you dare suggest rearrangement of stanzas to "help clarify the sense of chronology"? How do you edit genius? Anyone who has ever taught a poetry workshop is sure to see him or herself in this poem — and the next time he or she sets pen to student manuscript to comment on a student poem will surely chuckle, if not with embarrassment then certainly with self-consciousness!

Many of the poets included here are well known and widely published, whereas others are less known. Alphabetical arrangement by author seemed the least intrusive way to present the poems to readers. We included poems written in traditional and experimental forms, and tried to include poems in a variety of styles and tones: meditative, reflective, reverent and irreverent, parody, satirical, whimsical, improvisational, and serious. Many of the poems borrow freely from Dickinson's biography, and others imagine events from the poet's life. Many of the poets use lines from Dickinson's poems or letters as "triggers" for their inspiration. Most of the time, a poem's connection to Dickinson's life and work is direct and deliberate; at other times it appears less direct, even oblique, but there nonetheless. In her insightful essay on Dickinson entitled "Her Moment of Brocade: The Reconstruction of Emily Dickinson," the poet Alice Fulton writes of a "resistance to a Dickinsonian tradition in American letters" and that "Among scholars and general readers, [Dickinson's] eminence is taken for granted. But who among contemporary poets has been placed within a Dickinsonian context? Where are her heirs?" Included also, then, are poems that we believe bear this inheritance – not necessarily in their surface allusion to a Dickinson poem or biographical moment, but rather in their depths with the undeniable resonance of Dickinson's influence. These poems are like the currents that rush around our ankles when we are standing knee-deep in still water.

We surely have missed other fine poems inspired by the life and work of Emily Dickinson – unpublished poems, poems in little magazines and in collections, and even poems on the Web. We hope our readers will bring those poems to our attention. As is often the case with anthologies, space and budget limitations prevented us from including poems that we otherwise would have enjoyed including.

As editors, we take full responsibility for any errors in the collection. Should the collection go into a second printing or another edition, we will make every effort to correct errors we discover or those brought to our attention by readers.

Putting together this anthology has been like puzzling a riddle and editing genius. We would like to thank the many writers who were generous with their poetry and supportive with their enthusiasm, often suggesting leads for other poems and being patient with the editing process. We also would like to thank the many editors and publishers who helped arrange permissions to reprint many of the poems. Early on in our hunt for poems, we discovered a long-out-of-print chapbook titled *ED: Letters from the World*, edited by Marguerite Harris and published in 1971 by Corinth Books (New York). We were pleased to discover the collection and are delighted to include some of the poems that first appeared in the collection. Another source of contemporary poems about Emily Dickinson has been the *Emily Dickinson International Society Bulletin*, a publication of the Emily Dickinson International Society. The "Poet to Poet" feature in the *EDIS Bulletin* offers poets an opportunity to reflect – often in their own poems inspired by Dickinson – on the influence of Dickinson in their own work. We strongly encourage readers interested in the life and work of Emily Dickinson to subscribe to this first-rate, highly informative publication. Gary Stonum and Georgiana Strickland, editors and board members of the *EDIS Bulletin*, were helpful to us in locating poets and poems.

We are especially grateful for the help of Cheryl Petersmeyer and Charlene Duncan who, early on in the project, assisted us with typing the manuscript and organizing our files and correspondence into an efficient, workable coherency. We also would like to thank our friends and colleagues, especially David Young and William Zaranka, who helped us locate poems and authors. We are also grateful to Robert Bly for taking time from his busy life to write an introduction for the collection. Cara Moser of the Pennyroyal Press was especially helpful to us in obtaining the exquisite engraving of Emily Dickinson by Barry Moser. Holly Carver, editor of the University of Iowa Press, and her professional staff deserve a special thanks. Holly's excitement about the project early on, and her support and insight throughout the project, were especially meaningful to us as we collaborated and shaped the project with her in cyberspace. We are also grateful to our students and colleagues at Minnesota State University Moorhead who supported the project in numerous ways. We also thank Minnesota State University Moorhead for a Faculty Development Grant that helped us in the completion of the project.

# Why We Love Emily Dickinson

ROBERT BLY

Why do we love Emily Dickinson so much? She is always ready to say that everything has failed. With her pincers she goes around picking up sand grains of failure. One sand grain is enough to signal to her that her love affair has failed, that her effort to love God has failed, that her day's humility has failed, that she has fallen through her own standards and her desire, which seemed so huge a moment ago, is nothing.

She is warrior: she goes into battle covered with blood. This is not someone who stands around waiting for reinforcements to arrive. She doesn't want for a male minister to tell her it's time to travel toward God.

Shabistari the Sufi poet, said:

Everything is always aware of its own source
And so it is always making for the throne of the King.

That's what we like.

She is aware of her source! Hawthorne is aware of his ancestors' guilt and so he is always ready to testify in court. But Emily is ready to start on the road. "The person who loves her beginning knows her end." And so she is always writing about finding herself on the way to the mysterious mound of earth. She remembers that important day when she surmised that "the horses' heads were toward eternity." Well, what is the difference between beginning and end?

Everything is always aware of its source.
And so it is always making for the throne of the King.

We love her because she never declares she is closer to the goal than she was yesterday, and so she never leaves any of us behind. We're not sure how well we can love people who go too fast; we might be behind them. But Emily Dickinson is always behind us, and each day she starts out from her bed, which is no wider than her coffin will be, making for the throne of the King:

Rowing in Eden –
Ah, the Sea!
Might I but moor – Tonight –
In Thee!

# Visiting Emily

# "Miss Emily's Maggie" Remembers

JEAN BALDERSTON

*"I never saw the Sea —"*


But sure she saw the sea:
at Boston Harbor, when a girl.
Seemed teacup more than sea, she said.
She said Mount Auburn's graves made brinier sense,
that seeing all their marble rise like foam
made sea-change seem "rich and strange."
That was Mr. Shakespeare.
She would do that: knead bread and recite.
It helped the yeast to rise, she said.
She'd often go and murmur lines in the cupola.
I'd see her from the yard,
that is, I'd see a blur of white sway.
It came to me, the way she'd *list* up there —
Miss Emily knew the sea.
That would be Miss Emily,
to tell the Pelham hills to be
the breakers in her head.

# The Mystery of Emily Dickinson

MARVIN BELL

Sometimes the weather goes on for days
but you were different. You were divine.
While the others wrote more and longer,
you wrote much more and much shorter.
I held your white dress once: 12 buttons.
In the cupola, the wasps struck glass
as hard to escape as you hit your sound
again and again asking Welcome. No one.

Except for you, it were a trifle:
This morning, not much after dawn,
in level country, not New England's,
through leftovers of summer rain I
went out rag-tag to the curb, only
a sleepy householder at his routine
bending to trash, when a young girl
in a white dress your size passed,

so softly!, carrying her shoes. It must be
she surprised me – her barefoot quick-step
and the earliness of the hour, your dress –
or surely I'd have spoken of it sooner.
I should have called to her, but a neighbor
wore that look you see against happiness.
I won't say anything would have happened
unless there was time, and eternity's plenty.

# Your Birthday in Wisconsin You Are 140

JOHN BERRYMAN

'One of the wits of the school' your chum would say –
Hot diggity! – What the *hell* went wrong for you,
Miss Emily, – besides the 'pure & terrible' Congressman
your paralyzing papa, – and Mr Humphrey's dying
    & Benjamin's (the other reader)? . . .

Fantastic at 32 outpour, uproar, 'terror
since September, I could tell to none'
after your 'Master' moved his family West
and timidly to Mr Higginson:
    'say if my verse is alive.'

Now you wore only white, now you did not appear,
till frantic 50 when you hurled your heart
down before Otis, who would none of it
thro' five years for 'Squire Dickinson's cracked daughter'
    awful by months, by hours . . .

Well. Thursday afternoon, I'm in W———
drinking your ditties, and (dear) *they* are *alive*, –
more so than (bless her) Mrs F who teaches
farmers' red daughters & their beaux *my* ditties
    and yours & yours & yours!
    Hot diggity!

# Visiting Emily Dickinson's Grave with Robert Francis

ROBERT BLY

Robert Francis has moved, since his stroke, into town, and he takes me to the cemetery. A black iron fence closes the graves in, its ovals delicate as wine stems. They resemble those chapel windows on the main Aran island, made narrow in the fourth century so that not too much rain would drive in. . . . It is April, clear and dry. Curls of grass rise around the nearby gravestones.

The Dickinson house is not far off. She arrived here one day, at fifty-six, Robert says, carried over the lots between by six Irish laboring men, when her brother refused to trust her body to a carriage. The coffin was darkened with violets and pine boughs, as she covered the immense distance between the solid Dickinson house and this plot . . .

The distance *is* immense, the distances through which Satan and his helpers rose and fell, oh vast areas, the distances between stars, between the first time love is felt in the sleeves of the dress, and the death of the person who was in that room. . . . the distance between the feet and head as you lie down, the distance between the mother and father, through which we pass reluctantly.

*Exultation is the going*
*Of the inland soul to sea,*
*Past the houses, past the headlands*
*Into deep Eternity.*

Emily is sarcastic: "My family addresses an Eclipse every morning, which they call their 'Father.'"

As we leave the cemetery, Robert says, "The apartment is small, but I took it because I could see her grave from my window." He has given his life to seeing what is far away. He used to serve a visitor – in a small glass – wine made from his own dandelions. "Can you mistake us? . . . For this I have abandoned all my other lives."

# For Emily Dickinson

MARIANNE BORUCH

When I stood for a moment
in that white room, vines busy outside
at the screen, I thought
of the moth in you, the rich wool
it desired. I watched it
circle once, twice, nearing
the narrow bed, the little desk
though nothing was diminutive.

And I know what a lousy daughter knows,
those years ago I lived
not three blocks from your house – idiot child,
bone stubborn, never reading your poems much, never
keeping proper vigil. Regret has its
own insect life, that tedious hum
trapped in the head. It can't get out.

But your house was too high, set on a knoll,
a wedding cake crusted
with legend. Here, eat some, my teachers said.
Each one of them would marry you. Still, once
walking past, I invented flowers
for your garden: the dumb, sweet heliotrope, the dull hiss
of lupine, delphinium's brooding reach.
Among them, you stood right up
and squinted. You who noticed everything
made nothing of me, one of the stupid
and unborn, not even the color
of a leaf yet.

*Matty, here's freedom,* you told
your niece one ordinary day, locking the door of that room
behind you, locking both of you in.
My aunt once gave me such a box, a nest
of boxes really, all rushed wooden birds

and fish in a tangle, all intricately carved,
each opening into its secret smaller self.
I lost count quickly. Or maybe
there were seven. I looked up,
too amazed to tell her.

# Queen Recluse

LUCIE BROCK-BROIDO

If, then, the moon would be a good place to place the Jews,
Then I must stay here in a province of terrestrial jewelled
Heathens, I will stay at home & worshipping. With no promise
Of an afterlife, then I will comb the moors in rainy April
When the heathers are discolored by the rusts of a restless
Consumptive season, the stone walls of the parsonage ablaze
With little germs & breathe my brother's madness, his
Melancholias, take in the liquid punishments of eventual
Seclusion, a hand-bound bottle-green anonymous & fascicled
Collection of some Poetry in hand. Even the dog will die of age
Near me. Where would a Christian do her perishing? Monochrome
Life, a galaxy of light benigned in the planet's time it takes
To reach me wandering this rusted liquid earth of rain & rain, raking
Moors with metronomes of prayer. Earthly lesion, parish of my home.

# Emily Dickinson Attends a Writing Workshop

JAYNE RELAFORD BROWN

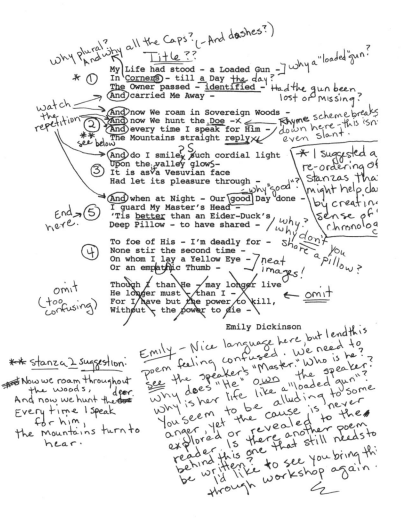

My Life had stood - a Loaded Gun -
In Corners - till a Day
The Owner passed - identified -
And carried Me Away -

And now We roam in Sovereign Woods -
And now We hunt the Doe -
And every time I speak for Him -
The Mountains straight reply -

And do I smile, such cordial light
Upon the Valley glows -
It is as a Vesuvian face
Had let its pleasure through -

And when at Night - Our good Day done -
I guard My Master's Head -
'Tis better than an Eider-Duck's
Deep Pillow - to have shared -

To foe of His - I'm deadly foe -
None stir the second time -
On whom I lay a Yellow Eye -
Or an emphatic Thumb -

Though I than He - may longer live
He longer must - than I -
For I have but the power to kill,
Without - the power to die -

Emily Dickinson

# Emily Dickinson's To-Do List
## Sum-Sum-Summertime

ANDREA CARLISLE

*Monday*
Figure out what to wear — white dress?

Put hair in bun
Bake gingerbread for Sue
Peer out window at passersby
Write poem
Hide poem

*Tuesday*
White dress? Off-white dress?
Feed cats
Chat with Lavinia
Work in garden
Write to T. W. H.

*Wednesday*
White dress or what?
Eavesdrop on visitors from behind door
Write poem
Hide poem

*Thursday*
Try on new white dress
Gardening — watch out for narrow fellows in grass!
Gingerbread, cakes, treats
Poems: Write and hide them

*Friday*
Embroider sash for white dress
Write poetry
Water flowers on windowsill
Hide everything

# Give Me Shoots, You Said

SIV CEDERING


If I were a monk of some other age, or nun,
I would write sonnets praising God
or tend a garden, where Madonna lilies grew tall
around a fountain. I would bake my love
into loaves of bread and say,
"The wine that wets my lips is the one
communion."
But I am a contemporary woman.
All day I walk with the feeling of your skin
upon my skin, mixing the blood of *you are*
and *I am*. The garden that I tend is all inside
and you the light. Everything
is pushing to get out. When you are gone,
I put my arms around myself
to keep the growing down.
I try to remember it is winter.
Seeds should sleep contented in the ground.
Bulbs should be self-contained temples,
ready to ring their bells
at appropriate times.
God, I'm afraid I am made of transparent stuff.
I don't mean the transparency of glass
but that of earth, ready to yield. The dust of what I am
might break, exposing
deep-rooted lilies that would leap and spire,
knowing you the fire of their sun.

"Give me shoots," you said, "from your gardens."

# Amherst

AMY CLAMPITT

*May 15, 1987*


The oriole, a charred and singing coal,
still burns aloud among the monuments,
its bugle call to singularity the same
unheard (she wrote) as to the crowd,
this graveyard gathering, the audience
    she never had.

Fame has its own dynamic, its smolderings
and ignitions, its necessary distance:
Colonel Higginson, who'd braved the cannon,
admitted his relief not to live near such
breathless, hushed excess (you cannot
    fold a flood,

she wrote, and put it in a drawer), such
stoppered prodigies, compressions and
devastations within the atom — *all this
world contains: his face* — the civil
wars of just one stanza. A universe
    might still applaud,

the red at bases of the trees (she wrote)
like mighty footlights burn, God still
looks on, his badge a raised hyperbole —
inspector general of all that carnage,
those gulfs, those fleets and crews
    of solid blood:

the battle fought between the soul and No
One There, no one at all, where cities
ooze away: unbroken prairies of air
without a settlement. On Main Street
the hemlock hedge grows up untrimmed,
    the light that poured

in once like judgment (whether it was noon
at night, or only heaven at noon, she wrote,
she could not tell) cut off, the wistful,
the merely curious, in her hanging dress discern
an ikon; her ambiguities are made a shrine,
    then violated;

we've drunk champagne above her grave, declaimed
the lines of one who dared not live aloud.
I thought of writing her (Dear Emily, though,
seems too intrusive, Dear Miss Dickinson too prim)
to ask, not without irony, what, wherever she
    is now, is made

of all the racket, whether she's of two minds
still; and tell her how on one cleared hillside,
an ample peace that looks toward Norwottuck's
unaltered purple has been shaken since
by bloodshed on Iwo Jima, in Leyte Gulf
    and Belleau Wood.

# Taking Off Emily Dickinson's Clothes

BILLY COLLINS

First, her tippet made of tulle,
easily lifted off her shoulders and laid
on the back of a wooden chair.

And her bonnet,
the bow undone with a light forward pull.

Then the long white dress, a more
complicated matter with mother-of-pearl
buttons down the back,
so tiny and numerous that it takes forever
before my hands can part the fabric,
like a swimmer's dividing water,
and slip inside.

You will want to know
that she was standing
by an open window in an upstairs bedroom,
motionless, a little wide-eyed,
looking out at the orchard below,
the white dress puddled at her feet
on the wide-board, hardwood floor.

The complexity of women's undergarments
in nineteenth-century America
is not to be waved off,
and I proceeded like a polar explorer
through clips, clasps, and moorings,
catches, straps, and whalebone stays,
sailing toward the iceberg of her nakedness.

Later, I wrote in a notebook
it was like riding a swan into the night,
but, of course, I cannot tell you everything —
the way she closed her eyes to the orchard,

how her hair tumbled free of its pins,
how there were sudden dashes
whenever we spoke.

What I can tell you is
it was terribly quiet in Amherst
that Sabbath afternoon,
nothing but a carriage passing the house,
a fly buzzing in a windowpane.

So I could plainly hear her inhale
when I undid the very top
hook-and-eye fastener of her corset

and I could hear her sigh when finally it was unloosed,
the way some readers sigh when they realize
that Hope has feathers,
that reason is a plank,
that life is a loaded gun
that looks right at you with a yellow eye.

# Dickinson

MARTHA COLLINS

Deep in the hills, in the noon sun,
through the white gate, through the white front door,
up the stairs to the room, and the white dress —

up the stairs, to the cupola,
where the turning world — the trees, the hills,
the hills beyond circumference — returned.

Is this what body comes to, then,
after the dinners, the talk, the wine,
hello, goodbye, is this the way,
most I, most who I am?

He was perfect muse, the god who was
and was not there. She had no mother,
she said, her mother was awe.

But awe was also muse, was house,
was hills, beyond the hills —

Mother, wife, the earth at last.
For us it goes the other way:

the deep green cave, the flesh
of love, the wings
of the white election —

# To Emily Dickinson

HART CRANE

You who desired so much — in vain to ask —
Yet fed your hunger like an endless task,
Dared dignify the labor, bless the quest —
Achieved that stillness ultimately best,

Being, of all, least sought for: Emily, hear!
O sweet, dead Silencer, most suddenly clear
When singing that Eternity possessed
And plundered momently in every breast;

— Truly no flower yet withers in your hand,
The harvest you descried and understand
Needs more than wit to gather, love to bind.
Some reconcilement of remotest mind —

Leaves Ormus rubyless, and Ophir chill.
Else tears heap all within one clay-cold hill.

# Amherst with Fries

PHILIP DACEY

When the bored cashier at Burger King
pauses as she takes my order to note
with at least a little wonder
how "Whopper" and "water" "sound alike,"
I say nothing except, "They do, don't they?"
but secretly rejoice to find alive where I least
expected it the spirit of poetry.

I want to kiss her, despite her ugliness
and nature so dwarfish she has to stand
on a stool to punch the register, for I'm thinking
of Emily Dickinson, absolute mistress
of the off-rhyme, her deliciously glancing blows
of sound, and know I'm talking to her sister.
If I'd add, "like 'pearl' and 'alcohol,'" I'm sure
she'd nod and go all dizzy, one more Inebriate of Air.

I want to invite her to my poetry workshop
at the local college or even to conduct one
immediately in this place – among the grease
and sickeningly sweet drinks tell her that
William Stafford said what she already
knows instinctively, how all words rhyme,
any two of them sounding more like each other
than either one of them sounds like silence,
that "burger" has an affinity, therefore, with
"Massachusetts," and language is always
and in any state the special of the day.

Beginning to feel as close to her as, say,
"Whopper" is to "water," I suddenly realize
that although few people full-rhyme
all people off-rhyme, that any one of them
is more at home with any other, or should be,
than either is with styrofoam cups or a plastic tray.

Of course I don't tell her all that I'm thinking –
some passions, ask Emily, are best concealed;
I only accept the fact that I'm order number five
and wait down the counter for what started all this
to arrive, thinking that here,
as the last years of the twentieth century
scrape America off the grill, shovelling it
into the stainless steel trenches
at either side, to be cleaned out later,
there's cause for hope in this minimum-
wage earner's surprising – even to her, I bet –
regard for what daily commercial use
has reduced to near invisibility: our life-
giving diet of vowel-and-consonant clusters,
including the two she grasped in her imagination
like a customer delicately picking up
his fry and contemplating it momentarily,
disinterestedly studying the shape and coloring,
feeling the texture under thumb and forefinger,
before closing his loving lips over it,
the way Emily closed her lips,
and her sister could as well have, over,
"I'm Nobody – Who are You – Are you Nobody, too?"

And as I'm eating like any other nobody,
I realize I'm enjoying, more than my Whopper,
the thought of this cashier at her post
playing the role of an intelligent ear,
a kind of subversive national weapon,
a uniformed and smiling stealth poet,
listening with great discrimination
as a line forms all day in front of her.

# Emily Dickinson and Gerard Manley Hopkins

MADELINE DeFREES

My notebook shows they took a formal cruise,
floated past bridges in the morning light.
From cliffs of fall to mid-Atlantic blues
they traveled fifteen knots the day her White
Election fell to his Ignatian news
of still pastures and feel-of-primrose night.
I owe my life to that New England nun
and triple locks the musing lover sprung.

In Amherst Emily prepared to risk it:
she scrawled some verse on napkins, tucked the wild
game in a hamper, doubled a batch of biscuit
dough and stepped over her father's threshold
while the old man napped. Too timorous to ask it
— he may have dreamed her docile as a child —
Gerard approved, leaving his Company behind
for her improbable liquor, out of his mind.

The world they charged led soon to a famous wreck:
both saw it looming off the coast of Wales.
The demure velvet ribbon about her neck
was not a leash, and cautionary tales
rang true. Her cries rose with the waves on deck,
the lioness again, breasting the gales
that left her adamant to write the letter
granting each heart its stone for worse or better.

The first three drafts were bitter as dark beer.
The next seemed overlong; the fifth, too frantic.
She made a couplet timed to disappear
the instant one considered it pedantic
and for the stricken lute of the sonneteer
a veiled refrain of grief become romantic.
Not one would do. She'd have to write in bed.
He found her there and straightway lost his head.

She showed Gerard where he would find his own
pale eyes inside the velvet-tethered locket.
Poor Emily! How else could she have known
he carried Whitman in his greatcoat pocket?
It's best, I think, to leave the pair alone
until their dull dough sours on the captain's docket.
In any case there's no communion service
when this bread's gone and Emily is nervous.

How could she give him up to any storm
after the voyage shared – those breathless dashes –
a line all stress, or nearly so, a form
impervious as slag, set free of ashes.
Let others rest in harbor, safe and warm.
They found their comfort in the cold sea crashes
the black west sent to beat the soldier's cave:
that Roman collar carried to the grave,

laid like a wreath over the unmarked vault
where bones of ghostly lovers washed ashore
on her white beach. The sand ground from basalt
by wind and wave in the skull's unquiet roar
was soft-sift now, though powerless to halt
the glassed descent from ecstasy and more.
These brief affairs we label mid-Victorian,
seduce the timid soul of wit's historian.

"Gerard," Emily wrote, under a sky all sunset,
"It's over – like a tune – the sad Campaign
of Sting and Sweet – will never be the one let
soar – The Auctioneer of Parting – bid the rain
rehearse the dew." Her pen assailed the runlet
crossing the intimate sheet with a purple stain,
my Grandmother Dickinson, dyed in the clerical woof,
was warped for good. I am the living proof.

# Sitting with Myself in the Seton Hall Deli at 12 O'clock Thursday Before I Read with the Great Poets at the Emily Dickinson Poetry Festival

TOI DERRICOTTE

1.

When I read with them, when I hear them,
I will know
I'm inferior.

2.

I don't like myself snivelling,
but I need to sit with myself & keep my poor self company.
I pity myself, who has come here to adore the great poets,
who
hates my miserable leaky cup, who
cannot concentrate, looks from this one to that,
sits in the seat shrunken down, crying
with the beauty of their words.
So close, but so far away!

3.

Self-pity, self-doubt, I acknowledge you.
I will not hate you.
You are part of me.
I will not push you away.
I will sit with you & keep you company.
I will have my hand on your heart.
I will not deny you.
I will not forget your grief.
You are my secret sister.
Are you afraid I will leave you in the dark?
Come with me into the room.
Whisper in my ear.
Put your tiny hand around my neck, those fat rosy fingers.
your body along my ribs, fit to me.
I can carry you monkey fashion,
your head a small cup on my neck.

4.

*for Ruth Stone*

In order to love women
you have to come to the Emily Dickinson Centennial
& hear Maxine Kumin say: "Emily, you are
a poet, you were. And
you lasted."
   In order to
last you must kiss the poet on the
back of her red head just as she
approaches the podium, weak, un-
believing. Un-
believable how confidence can come from
tasting the Parmesan placed as a gift
on top of the deli soup, the
final blessing.
Compare yourself with the
greats, the
dead, the Pulitzers, the
scholars, the housewives.
It doesn't matter whether you came by
car or bus, whether you walk on a lame
ankle. It doesn't matter if you have not
been promoted or
if you must first
sit in the ladies' room with a blank
notebook and wonder if you should use the paper
to wipe the seat.
   Emily waited to be famous
till all her friends were dead.
Good girl! I wish my friends
would do the same!


5.

because she could not say
rape, i say rape
because she could not say
penis, i say penis
because she could not say

breast & mean that sexual rising
i say breast & mean
*that* sexual rising

"Tell all the truth, but tell it slant."
We don't have time to slant. This morning
on the radio: "Invest in an IRA," Yes,
but will we be alive to collect?
We are her daughters.
But could she accept us?
Was her white
a put-down of the black?
Is she ready for
all these various voices?
I wish we could hear all the writings from people's notebooks.

# Emily Dickinson

RICHARD EBERHART

He saw a laughing girl
And she said to him,
I must take a man
Toward eternity.

Her flesh was soft and fleet,
Her mouth was like a pose,
And a spiritual drift
Played about her flowing clothes.

She said she could not be
An evidence of the free
Unless she left her body
To become immortality.

She took him in the main
And held him in a trance
Who never knew for thirty years
Whether she was the dancer or the dance.


II

She was the highest mark
To which he set a snare.
He held her in his clutch
But she vanished in the air.

She departed with the years
And rode upon her destiny
While he was retained much
In the hold of mystery.

Now he must forswear
The roll of reality
And must admit the truth
Of what he cannot see.

She is gone with the wind
And he is gone with the weather.
Only in spirituality
Can they be said to be together.

Pretend to the flesh,
But the flesh will fall away.
In timeless uselessness
Love can have a stay.

He thought he held her
When passion was high.
Time brings her to him
In a long, in a wind-drawn sigh.

# Homage to Dickinson

LYNN EMANUEL

I've never longed for the annulments of Heaven,
nor for Hell, that orgy of repenting,
but have wanted the loneliness of this
slender room and bed, the cool neatness
of being dead: to be reduced, cleaned out,
a manageable mess, nothing left but knobs
and buttons, the skull an empty crock,
the pelvis a washed plate, the ribs laid
tidily, side by side. And I would be gone,
not that stern black dress, not that thing
with the Bible on her breasts. I would be
nothing but one narrow room of sepulcher,
one barred window where traffic never brings
its soot, the ear clean and empty as a scrubbed cup,
the tongue at rest and I, free at last, the window
of myself cast open, and all the sweet lament
of mourners throbbing in the distance, the angels'
white blouses pinned to the line of the horizon.
I would be alone, alone, in my maidenly
tomb, my own woman. Finally. And forever.

# Vermont Summer

DAVE ETTER


Walking this morning through the forest,
cool and damp and sweet with rot,
I find red and yellow mushrooms
that are soft and rubbery to my touch.
And I find silver speckled stones
stuck in sand by the skipping stream.
And I find the skin of a birch tree
hanging loose and curly from the trunk.
And on a stump in a flower of sun
I find a frog no bigger than my eye.

And I think of you now, Emily,
knowing that you in your sure-footed joy
would know what secrets are revealed here
by mushroom, stone, birch bark, frog.

Yours was the harvest of small mysteries.

# A Letter for Emily Dickinson

ANNIE FINCH


Like me, you used to write while baking bread,
propping a sheet of paper by the bins
of salt and flour, so if your kneading led
to words, you'd take them, looping their thin shins
in your black writing, as they sang to be free.
You captured those quick birds relentlessly,
yet kept a slow, sure mercy in your deeds,
leaving them room to peck and hunt their seeds
in the white cages your vast iron art
·had made by moving books, and lives, and creeds.
I take from you as you take me apart.

When I cut words you might never have said
into fresh patterns, pierced in place with pins,
ready to hold them down with my own thread,
they change and twist sometimes, their color spins
loose, and your spider generosity
lends them from language that will never be
free of you after all. My sampler reads,
"called back." It says "she scribbled out these screeds."
It calls, "she left this trace, and now we start,"
in stitched directions following the leads
I take from you, as you take me apart.

# Emily Dickinson in Boston, 1864 – 65

RICHARD FOERSTER

*. . . the calls at the Doctor's are painful, and dear Vinnie,*
*I have not looked at the Spring.*
*— E. D. from Cambridge, May 1864*

That daguerreotype, with its strabismic gaze,
skews my understanding of her miracle years,
when all heaven seemed to spin on her lathe
and the work fell solid, by the hundreds.

All her life she'd slowly been shutting doors,
until striding home one day through a spume
of widow's lace (or loosestrife or asters)
she'd had enough, and turned the lock, like so,

and doffed her wide-brimmed hat without a flourish.
But what did it mean to select the white austerities,
to know the world through an atlas circumscribed
and limned on a bedroom's frost-etched panes,

to spar each day with "that little god with epaulettes"
and win? The niceties of legend blanch against the plate:
Her right eye pins us to the paradox of serenity
(how long did she have to hold that pose?); the left eye

strays to confront some hidden radiance – a terror,
she later called it – lurking on vision's periphery.
Symptoms: Foci out of sync, solids ghosted,
the gentlest lights clinging like burrs, ciliary shudders,

all the small betrayals plus that final voltage:
whole foundries of print smeared across the page. Surely
more than panic spurred her into poetry's rolling fires
for those three years. . . . But strolling here, toward dusk,

through the Public Garden – past the swan boats
nuzzling their piers, among the quiet, bivouacked flocks
hoarding the last fugitive rays – I want to imagine her,
here, sure-footed, beyond the squinched regime

of her doctor's care, beyond the clotted vacancies
of the Charles, come to this shadowed calm, this willed
clarity among the geraniums' percussive reds, and yet
it's dislocated fear I sense – a blur – and hurry on.

# Two Ghosts

ROBERT FRANCIS

Amherst. Dark hemlocks conspiring at the First Church midway between the Mansion on Main Street and the back entrance (the escape door) of the Lord Jeffery Inn. Between one and two after midnight.

R  Someone is here. Angelic? Or demonic?

E  Someone less than someone.

R  Emily?

E  How could you divine me?

R  An easy guess, you who were ghost while living
   and haunting us ever since.

E  A ghost to catch a ghost?

R  A poet to catch a poet.

E  And you – you must be the Robert who said:
   "The petal of the rose it was that stung."
   Or did *I* say it?

R  We both have said it now.

E  Sweet the bee – but rose is sweeter –
   Quick his sting – but rose stings deeper –
   Bee will heal – rose petal – never

R  You talk of bees who were yourself white moth.

E  Seldom flitting so far from home.
   Oftener the other way to touch my stone.
   Have you seen it?

R  *Called Back?*

E  The stone keeps calling me back.

R  I would have cut a different epitaph.
   *Called on. Called ahead.*

E  But on and back are both one now, aren't they?

R  My stone is not a stone but a heap, a pile –

E  Why should immortality be so stony?

R  – a mass, a mausoleum, a mock mountain
   over there. Have you seen?

E  Oh, I took *that* for a factory or fort.

R  Fort of learning, factory of scholars.
   And my name cut deep in granite. Have you seen?

E  I never dared to go so far – so near.

R "Less than someone," you said. I say,
"More than someone." You are a name now, Emily.
E Why do they hunt me so?
R The scholar-scavengers?
E Once I could hide but now
they try my mind, they pry
apart my heart.
R We were both hiders. You
in your father's house. I
in the big buzzing world.
I craved to be understood
but feared being wholly known.
E You said, "Anything more than the truth
would have seemed too weak."
R And you, "Truth like ancestors' brocades
can stand alone." I should say truth
is not the dress but the naked lady.
E Or naked gentleman.
R Have it as you will.

(A tower clock strikes two)

R There's truth for you.
To tell the truth
is all a clock can do.
E But clocks are human — like us all —
They err — grow ill — and finally fail.
R They never lie intentionally.
E Why did you say, "Nature's first green is gold?"
Some buds, yes, but the buds of beech are cinnamon,
and the swamp maple — but need I tell you?
R And why — why did you say:
"Nature rarer uses yellow than another hue?"
Think of the dandelions, Emily, the fields
of solid yellow. Think of the forsythias
and buttercups. The sugar maple's pendant blooms,
the cowslips, cinquefoil, golden Alexanders,
the marigolds and all the goldenrods.
Witch-hazel and October trees: beech, elm,
maple, popple, apple!

E  Why did Emerson, your Emerson, my Emerson, say,
   "Succory to match the sky?" Imagine!
R  Your lines that haunt me most —
E  What are they?
R  "After great pain a formal feeling comes.
   The nerves sit ceremonious like tombs."
E  Oh! Oh!
R  "After great pain —"
E  And that line of yours:
   "Weep for what little things could make them glad."
R  I was writing of children.
E  We are all children.
R  Laugh at what little things could make them weep.
E  Can make us all weep. Were you a believer?
R  I took the dare to believe. I made myself
   believe I believed. And you?
E  Two angels strove like wrestlers in my mind:
   one belief, one disbelief.
R  "After great pain —"
E  Oh!
R  Emily? Emily!

# Of Women Who Wear White

ALICE FRIMAN

Like a farm girl
   practicing ballet,
      the klutzy sycamore

Stuns us with her pose. So too
   the blotchy bride
      pausing at aisle end

Before her long waft down.
   It is the white.
      The libidinous

Chastity of it.
   The Dover Cliffs and crown
      of any wardrobe.

It's the power suit.
   The Moby D. of *haute couture.*
      The one decision made

In defiance of good sense
   and menses.
      And no smirk of April

Mincing the park in pastel
   can eclipse the thunder
      of its speech.

Tell me, Lady of Amherst,
   shawled wonder, who
      is heir to your scraps?

Who gets the leftovers?
   Lawn and trim, snippets
      of eyelet – the white wink

Of Election?
    Every genius in America is out
        beating the bushes for your

Sewing basket.
    They know your habits,
        your penchant for cache —

Those little stitched-paper
    Everests
        you stashed away in a chest

The world's black needle
    wobbling to North
        would turn pearl to find.

# Wonder Bread

ALICE FULTON

*You asked me what my flowers said — then they*
*were disobedient — I gave them messages.*
*— Emily Dickinson, Letter #187*

What eucharist of air and bland

was this nation raised on? No one understood
my funny flowers — and Darwin —

Darwin was regarded as a charlatan.
Few viewers think

evolution is the truth.
My flowers *were* absurd.

Snips of sugar. Snails with spice.
Puppy dogs. Tales. Everything.

Nice!

But why did I admire nature so?
Was it that I liked

the absence of a Master
neuron in the brain —

the absence of a Master
cell in embryos —

the nothing in the way of
center that would hold?

What causes less comfort
than wonder?

What — does not console?

# Emily's Bread

SANDRA GILBERT

*1857 Emily's bread won a prize at the annual Cattle Show.*
*1858 Emily served as a judge in the Bread Division of the Cattle Show.*
— *John Malcolm Brinnin, "Chronology,"*
  Selected Poems of Emily Dickinson


Inside the prize-winning blue-ribbon loaf of bread,
there is Emily, dressed in white,
veiled in unspeakable words,
not yet writing letters to the world.

No, now she is the bride of yeast,
the wife of the dark of the oven,
the alchemist of flour, poetess of butter,
stirring like a new metaphor in every bubble

as the loaf begins to grow.
Prosaic magic, how it swells,
like life, expanding, browning
at the edges, hardening.

Emily picks up her pen, begins to scribble.
Who'll ever know? "This is my letter
to the world, that never. . . ."
Lavinia cracks an egg, polishes

the rising walls with light. Across
the hall the judges are making notes:
firmness, texture, size, flavor.
Emily scribbles, smiles. She knows it is

the white aroma of her baking skin
that makes the bread taste good.
Outside in the cattle pen the blue-ribbon heifers
bellow and squeal. Bread means nothing to them.

They want to lie in the egg-yellow sun.
They are tired of dry grain, tired of grooming and love.
They long to eat the green old meadow
where they used to live.

# Emily Dickinson's Room, Main Street, Amherst

BARRY GOLDENSOHN

Down through the cross of her windows
facing the West she saw
her father interpose
his hat, shoulders, shoes,
as he came or went or strolled
under the high-limbed trees;
and later her brother Austin
dally with Mabel Todd
under the same tall trees —
her shutters were always open —
their silent legible gestures
of intimate conversation,
one face obtruding, pressing
one listening looking down;
and the children crouch on the lawn
to watch as the puppy squats;
and the cat brace its legs
into a panting scaffold
to hoist a stubborn mole.
To the South she saw the street
through two uncurtained windows:
the long-legged fellow in black
ministering to the dead
reel the thread of his rounds;
the fire volunteers
in ceremonious panic
clamor out to the farms;
the farmers ride their wagons
that screech under flax and corn
and roped by the neck behind
the doomed steer low
his way to the abattoir;
but mostly the garden change

from crocus to tulip to rose,
their cohorts dying in ranks
yet coming and coming again
till driven to sleep by snow
and locked into place by ice.

# "Who Goes to Dine Must Take His Feast"

DAVID GRAHAM

The way a horse knows,
the moment he is reined around a bend,
that it is home now to the barn,
I feel the car shiver around me and quicken.
Ears of corn just beyond my taillights
begin to tremble in my wake.
Roadsigns seem familiar, then true,
and finally sympathetic.
I know that over this forest, surely,
in a house set back behind maples
a light is on in an upstairs window.
I know that house I have never seen:
bats and nighthawks flash
across the window light, and if she sees
she is fixed as I am fixed
in this landmark of my arrival.

# Teaching Emily Dickinson

RACHEL HADAS


What starts as one more Monday morning class
merges to a collective Dickinson,
separate vessels pooling some huge truth
sampled bit by bit by each of us.

She sings the pain of loneliness for one.
Another sees a life of wasted youth;
then one long flinching from what lay beneath
green earth; last, pallid peerings at the stone

she too now knows the secret of.

                              Alone,
together, we'd decipher BIRD   SOUL   BEE
dialect humdrum only until heard
with the rapt nervy patience, Emily,
you showed us that we owed you. One small bird
opens its wings. They spread. They cover us:
myriad lives foreshortened into Word.

# The Impossible Marriage

DONALD HALL


The bride disappears. After twenty minutes of searching
we discover her in the cellar, vanishing against a pillar
in her white gown and her skin's original pallor.
When we guide her back to the altar, we find the groom
in his slouch hat, open shirt, and untended beard
withdrawn to the belltower with the healthy young sexton
from whose comradeship we detach him with difficulty.
O never in all the meetinghouses and academies
of compulsory Democracy and free-thinking Calvinism
will these poets marry! – O pale, passionate
anchoret of Amherst! O reticent kosmos of Brooklyn!

# Spelunking

LOLA HASKINS

Our flames reach very short.
Only the thinnest of us pass
the squeeze. Dark is rising
up our legs. We are off the
map, and cold. The one who
holds the clearest light is

Emily. We see the lengthening
fingers of rock, how water
makes its slow difference.
Her arm falls to her side.
The moving beam glistens
on Emily's white dress.

# Letter to Miss Dickinson

WILLIAM HEYEN


I awoke this morning far from Amherst,
scents of your chaste
bosom's crushed flowers still

lingering – your hair tight, your thin,
eyes precise as your kiss
behind my eyes. . . .

In the uncertain light I'd torn
the white, grass-
length dress

of your spinsterhood.
The air choked me
with jonquils and roses:

Your breasts were marble,
Your tongue iams of passion
and statuary stone.

# The Unnaming

EDWARD HIRSCH

*Amherst, 1860*


She walked through the house, taking away its names.
The high ceilings will no longer be called ceilings,
She thought, and the parlors will no longer be parlors.

There will be no more bedchambers or sitting rooms,
No more Sheraton bureaus, Franklin stoves, cherry-wood tables.
There would be no more time for commonplace aspirations

As she moved through the halls in a rapture of unmaking,
Withdrawing the designations, taking down doors and windows,
The heavy stairs she had climbed so many times before,

Holding the banister and dreaming of a carpenter
Who had carved the boards from a sacrificial tree
So she could go back and forth to a white study.

She took courage from Eve's deleting of the names
Adam had given the beasts, haunting Eden
By returning the animals to their first splendor

And treating the garden as a page for revisions.
She took heart from a snowfall blanketing the earth,
An oblivion outside matching the oblivion within.

She, too, moved through a garden of cancellations
(*No more monarchies of Queen Anne's lace,* she chanted
To herself, *no more dead elms branching into heaven*)

And that was when she felt the dizzying freedom
Of a world cut loose from the affixed Word or words,
Appallingly blank, waiting to be renamed.

# For Emily Dickinson

PATRICIA Y. IKEDA

*she being too much for life   the rare person with no need to travel   the countries*
*split their horizons   the space inside her   felt like death*

*always a struggle between hunger and surfeit   who could have taken a world so*
*charged?   out on a walk, the explosion of the chestnut tree   the eye blazes*
*blossoms*

Her plain, straightforward face. I imagine long skirts, tightlaced boots. Who would think of her as inebriate of air   debauchee of dew? She knew the pure high of being, she kept it all her life. What consciousness and the imagination circumscribe is all we need. More than enough.

She stands by the cupboard, putting cups away. She holds the cup in two hands, looking down into it as if reading miniscule script printed around the rim. She stands on tip-toe, reaching for the shelf above her head, and gives the cup a little push forward. The cup falls. She slowly leans down, brushes aside the slivers of china, picks up the handle, turns it in the light.

The snow is falling. She is watching.

A fresh, cool pear on a small plate. She picks up the little silver fruit knife, puts it down, takes a large bite. She holds the juice in her mouth, swallows and looks around laughing. She writes her brother Austin:   you *must* have pears.

She did not burn them before she died, she did not leave any note to explain their existence. She knew there was a need for them. She felt within herself the amazing vector of eternity and knew it was her own force.

Her last letter: Little Cousins, – Called back.

Emily

*because she knew it    her hands were twisting    she wondered who was at the door*
*a black carriage jolting around a dusty corner    tassels swinging    she inside with*
*that genteel bone-man death    turning sunsets inside out    never a seam*
*to show*


*she sat invisibly in the cool dark hall    the piano was being played    she plunges*
*into the dense liqueur    the honey comb    Home    don't surface for air — at the end*
*that intense sweetness is bitter    that white fire    frost*

# Amherst: One Day, Five Poets: Part II

SHIRLEY KAUFMAN

The cupola is a windowed cage
at the top. The Holyoke Range
floats in the sky at twilight
and three half-dead wasps
blown in by the wind
jerk at my feet.
They can't get out again.
They wobble against the glass
And fall.

     Pale walls
the pale tatami floor.
Pearl jail she called it.
Safe as the inside of a shell.
Or wicker basket on her window sill.

She used to fill
it with her own warm gingerbread
and lower it to the children down below.

There is the recipe in her small script:
molasses sugar flour.
A branch of pear tree starts
to shine from the dark
the way a live thing moves
out of the stone
a hand releases to the light.

She wanted to know
if her poems breathed.

# Emily Dickinson Leaves a Message to the World, Now That Her Homestead in Amherst Has an Answering Machine

X. J. KENNEDY

Because I could not stop for Breath
Past Altitudes – of Earth –
Upon a reel of Tape I leave
Directions to my Hearth –

For All who will not let me lie
Unruffled in escape –
Speak quickly – or I'll intercept
Your Message with – a Beep.

Though often I had dialed and rung
The Bastion of the Bee –
The Answer I had hungered for
Was seldom Home – to me –

# The Deconstruction of Emily Dickinson

GALWAY KINNELL

The lecture had ended when I came in,
and the professor was answering questions.
I do not know what he had been doing with her
poetry, but now he was speaking of her
as a victim of reluctant male publishers.
When the questions dwindled, I put up my hand.
I said the ignorant meddling of the Springfield *Daily Republican*
and the hidebound response of literary men,
and the gulf between the poetic wishfulness
then admired and her own harsh knowledge,
had let her see that her poems
would not be understood in her time;
and therefore, passionate to publish,
she vowed not to publish again. I said
I would recite a version of her vow,

> Publication – is the Auction
> Of the Mind of Man –

but before I could, the professor broke in.
"Yes," he said, "'the Auction' — 'auction,' from *augere, auctum*, to
   augment, to author . . ."
"Let's hear the poem!" "The poem!" several women,
who at such a moment are more outspoken than men, shouted,
but I kept still and he kept going.
"In *auctum* the economy of the signifier is split, revealing an uncon-
   scious collusion in the bourgeois commodification of consciousness. While our author says 'no,' the unreified text says
   'yes,' yes?"
He kissed his lips together and turned to me
saying, "Now, may we hear the poem?"
I waited a moment for full effect.
Without rising to my feet, I said,
"Professor, to understand Dickinson
it may not always be necessary to uproot her words.
Why not, first, try *listening* to her?

Loyalty forbids me to recite her poem now."
No, I didn't say that — I realized
she would want me to finish him off with one wallop.
So I said, "Professor, I thought you
would welcome the words of your author.
I see you prefer to hear yourself speak."
No, I held back — for I could hear her
urging me to put outrage into my voice
and substance into my argument.
I stood up so that everyone might see
the derision in my smile. "Professor," I said,
"you live in Amherst at the end of the twentieth century.
For you 'auction' means a quaint event
where somebody coaxes out the bids
on butter churns on a summer Saturday.
Forget etymology, this is history.
In Amherst in 1860 'auction' meant
the slave auction, you dope!"
Well, I didn't say that either,
although I have said them all,
many times, in the middle of the night.
In reality, I stood up and recited the poem
like a schoolboy called upon in class.
My voice gradually weakened, and the women
who had called out for the poem
now looked as though they were thinking
of errands to be done on the way home.
When I finished, the professor smiled.
"Thank you. So, what at first some of us may have taken as a simple
     outcry, we all now see is an ambivalent, self-subversive text."
As people got up to go, I moved
into that sanctum within me where Emily
sometimes speaks a verse, and listened
for a sign of how she felt, such as,
"Thanks — Sweet — countryman —
for wanting — to Sing out — of Me —
after all that Humbug." But she was silent.

# Still Life with Riddle

TOM KOONTZ

*There are that resting, rise.*
*— Emily Dickinson*


It's something there behind the light blue-bottled
buildings and imperfect fruit. Some spillage
of the red upon the cloth, black in the pinks
igniting up and down the street. It's in the key of
*ai,* composed at the piano by the "private" woman
in the room above. We hear her in the distance
at odd hours, qualifying notes, repealing chords.
Like music to be danced on by the blind, while
Uncle Max is telling us again his story: tanks
parked in the wheat field one bright morning.
Sylvie wonders is it war. Paralysis of knowing
any step you take can detonate. The air drips
to a pool of pain, augmented to a faith, inverted
toward itself, despair. She glances toward the door.
At least that's how we see her. Bandaged fingers
buttoning a scale of words, words pressed upon
her tongue by darkness. Or one afternoon, snow
piled against the garbage bags, all stop.
She feels skies tip, let cities slip, the soldier earth
gone quiet in the din. Those pinks will soon
be lighting up again. She's at the window.
Buildings pouring blue like stones. A perfect
orange rolling past the edge. She listens
for a bell. Sustains the chord with white. Now
drops the *i.*

# After the Poetry Reading

MAXINE KUMIN

*for Marie Howe*

If Emily Dickinson lived in the 1990s
and let herself have sex appeal
she'd grow her hair wild and electric
down to her buttocks, you said. She'd wear
magenta tights, black ankle socks
and tiny pointed paddock boots.

Intrigued, I saw how Emily'd
master Microsoft, how she'd
fax the versicles that Higginson
advised her not to print to MS.
APR and Thirteenth Moon.

She'd read aloud at benefits
address the weavers' guild
the garden club, the anarchists
Catholics for free choice
welfare moms, the Wouldbegoods
and the Temple Sinai sisterhood.

Thinking the same thing, silent
we see Emily flamboyant.
Her words for the century to come
are pithy, oxymoronic.
Her fly buzzes me all the way home.

# Emily Dickinson's Sestina for Molly Bloom

BARBARA F. LEFCOWITZ


At times I almost believed it: madness
the only way to say yes,
to stumble into shapes of night
that gape open
like abandoned wells –
This would work like no other

disguise – yet I chose another
route, neither mad
nor well
enough to shout yes!
when morning scissor-blades opened
my sack of night

full of valentines to death – Night
whose curve of darkness I preferred to other
hours' slanting light that would open
all my closed lives – not the madly
flowered darkness that would make *you* say yes!
But – I might as well

admit it – the well-
sealed kind of night
where I could nod yes
to another
sputter of benign madness
from the loaded gun of an open

wound whose red opening
was never stanched well
enough; if only I hadn't feared the mad
shudder-burst & bloom demanded by your night
I would have become another
woman, spread open like a figtree in my father's
    northern garden, Yes

or — yes!
a house with its shutters open
to another
throng of lovers climbing my well-
flowered hair night after night,
all Amherst going mad,

its quartz contentment split open by the pulsing night —
Molly, as well become you as another —
Yes, and my heart going like mad and yes saying yes
    I will yes!

# When I Read a Review of the John Travolta Film, Michael

LYN LIFSHIN

and that "Emily Dickinson once said
that hope is a thing with feathers but
*Michael* is the hopeless thing with
feathers, an archangel who scratches
his crotch a lot, loves a good smoke
and can't keep his hands off women
but does have real wings, shedding
feathers," I think she'd double up
and collapse laughing. She'd have
liked Travolta's muscular arms tho
thought the plot a little goofy. If
anyone could appreciate a twist on
the devil and an arch angel, Emily
would be the one. She hadn't much
use for the bible thumpers. The only
angels she saw were in the woods
she'd been warned there were snakes
in. We'd go out and curl under the
darkest jade and howl at warnings
of poisonous flowers. Sometimes
we both got dragged to church.
Emily never prayed, except once
or twice. For Higginson. You know
when he went off to war, we giggled
about the supernatural, about witches
in the pond, werewolves in the orchard.
She felt like a gnome some days,
an old spirit, a psychic who foretold
a friend's injury by writing *Procession
of Flowers*. A John Travolta angel
with cigarette stained finger tips and
a devil laugh would have meant more,
been more real to Emily than any litany,
any psalms or hymns

# Emily Dickinson

MICHAEL LONGLEY

Emily Dickinson, I think of you
Wakening early each morning to write,
Dressing with care for the act of poetry.
Yours is always a perfect progress through
Such cluttered rooms to eloquence, delight,
To words – your window on the mystery.

By christening the world you live and pray –
Within those lovely titles is contained
The large philosophy you tend towards:
Within your lexicon the birds that play
Beside your life, the wind that holds your hand
Are recognised. Your poems are full of words.

In your house in Amherst Massachusetts,
Though like love letters you lock them away,
The poems are ubiquitous as dust.
You sit there writing while the light permits –
While you grow older they increase each day,
Gradual as flowers, gradual as rust.

# In the Flesh

LEE McCARTHY

I am tired of males swearing undying love for Emily Dickinson, praising her with a tongue usually reserved for Saturday night. I protest it each time. *Her poems suffer the confines of her life,* I say. *Think what she could have been, given Venice, Paris, a baby, emeralds in her ears.*

*Amherst was the cultural center of the country then. And she had two affairs,* is the answer back. His mouth wallows in its wine.

*Ah, well, I say, that's definite fulfillment.* I hear the woolen scratch of agreement in his jacket sleeves. *We're talking about a woman,* I add, *who would sit on the upper steps, hold her sister's hand, and talk to her married judge who had to stand in the livingroom next to the staircase out of view. When she couldn't take the pressure anymore, she'd flee to her room.*

*So?* he says. I blow smoke across the porch. *Flee to her room and write marvelous poems.* His words stroke together like oars set against the current of smoke. *She didn't need anyone.*

*That's pitiful. She could have been normal, gone to parties. Agape's too much by itself. We need eros, foam on the beer, cork in the bottom of the glass. Loved by a man, she'd have been Shakespeare, Dostoievski. Those pitiful asparagus poems. Those pitifully beautiful poems.*

He reiterates the affairs.

*That's not sleeping next to someone's back for twenty years,* I say.

*Normalcy would have ruined her,* he swears.

*You'd like to believe that,* I say and rub my lonely back against the rocker where I slump. We pause into silence.

*What are you thinking about?* he asks, as if by a staircase.

*About how I'm right but can't prove it.* He adjusts his jaunty hat which I'm half in love with. *All of you adore her now it does no good. I'd like to meet one man with enough sense to love her in the flesh.*

I count my buttons.

The last one hangs by a thread.

*Her ears weren't pierced,* he says.

# The Most Emily of All

MEDBH McGUCKIAN

When you dream wood I dream water.
When you dream boards, or cupboard,
I dream a lake of rain, a race sprung
from the sea. If you call out 'house' to me
and I answer 'library', you answer me
by the very terms of your asking,
as a sentence clings tighter
because it makes no sense.

Your light hat with the dark band
keeps turning up; you pull it right
down over your head and run the fingers
of your right hand up and down
in a groove on the door panel. A finger
going like this into my closed hand
feels how my line of life turns back
upon itself, in the kind of twilight
before the moon is seen.

A verse from a poem by Lermentov
continually goes round
in my head. A full ten days
has elapsed since I started my
'You can go or stay' letter, increasingly
without lips like the moon that night,
a repercussive mouth made for nothing,
and used for nothing.
just let me moisten your dreamwork
with the lower half of the letter,
till my clove-brown eyes beget a taller blue.

# In and Come In

ARCHIBALD MacLEISH

Stupid? Of course that older lot were stupid.
Any up-to-date, in poet
knows the bloody world was made for woe
and life for death and man is either dolt or dupe,

but those old locals never seemed to learn.
Emerson unlocked the tomb
and stood and stared at what had once been human,
once been his, and made that entry in his journal.

Whitman, in the stinking wards, uncovered
dead men's faces when the squad
came round at night and morning for the bodies,
but not to rage at death – to kiss them with his love.

Emily, although she said she wrote
as boys beside a graveyard whistle,
pressed no terrified finger to her wrist:
what frightened Emily was joy, the robin's note.

And later, when the word was Tragic Vision
haunting thickets of despair –
beckets of all the boredom flesh is heir to –
Frost went walking off alone in his derision.

Too ignorant to know what nightfall meant,
or why the thrush calls when the stars begin,
he told the weeping world he'd not come in
(even if asked, he said, and he hadn't been)
to mope among the hemlocks and lament.

He was out for stars, he told them, with that Yankee grin.
Stupid? Like all the rest: he didn't know.

And yet there's something *does* know in that poem.

# The Path Between Houses

JAY MEEK

Some nights there is a lamp burning when the house next door is quiet, and other nights the branches blowing up against the seasoned clapboards seem to shake the light to numbness. It is unremarkable, this scratchiness where bare branches open and close a path worn down almost to habit. And such goodness within a family, such indentured love – unremarkable. For they were born to duty, two sisters who attended their father and mother, a brother who left his wife's good bed. And so the path between their houses he took at night, they the next morning, tracking the wet leaves back and forth between two kitchens where women for another year polished their stories with silence, and looked out a window at the dark house next to their own.

That darkness, where the wind blows, see, that is where a word goes, there, and there, where everything is erased as the branches blow back and forth, that is where you have to fit a word for what cannot otherwise be said. And the silence that has numbed you: that is where you place the sad light with its bitter civilities, and shadows, the betrayal in your own stiff heart.

# Emily Dickinson in Hell

PETER MEINKE


How flat — as a democracy —
I wondered    entering
and seeing row on ragged row
unrav'ling like a sleeve

with no distinctions or — demands —
to pry the fearful eye
and none but Weather hanging there
across an absent sky

I looked for instruments and coal
machines whose teeth reflect
a terrifying gleam — to those
who suffer from Defect

I looked for friends or enemies
but only sapless trees
breathed meagerly in Emptiness
between the heated seas

until I shrieked in Agony
beneath a sycamore —
and peered deep in its branches
to find my Father — there

# A Love Poem for Emily Dickinson

BRUCE MEYER

I dreamt of your black house
where shadows hung like words,
where wind kept simple secrets
like flightless humming birds

until the house became a poem
that had no words or lines
and everything that entered it
was haunted by small designs.

The door was shaped like lips,
and windows formed a heart
but the hearth was cold as silence
and the house soon fell apart.

You will pass it in the meadow
where lovers hand in hand
walk out at the break of starlight
and kiss in the mortified land.

# Emily's Words

LESLIE MONSOUR

Unsquandered, sure and quiet as a root,
She stayed at home all dressed in pleated white,
And accurately weighed the brain of God,
The sum of acts not carried out. Unwed,
That she not be divided, she stayed whole,
And heard the sound the tooth makes in the soul.
A little knife that cuts through at a slant,
Her voice, a child's, ungendered, wasn't meant
For "Our Fathers" murmured under Sunday trees,
But rang like axe strokes on the frozen seas.
"Called back," she wrote, the mourners treading so,
That from her gypsy face a light broke through.
She died in May, and one thing struck them all:
The coffin was astonishingly small.

# JℓD/ℰD

AÍFE MURRAY

*for Barbara Guest*

*HD was born September 10, 1886 in Bethlehem, four months after ED died in Amherst. Did ED's soul travel southwest toward Nisky Hill. Is there only one woman poet in the world at a time, each a reincarnation of one that came before. Or are we "aspects" of each other as Durga is of Kali is of Radha. Dickinson of course is a reincarnation of Phillis Wheatley. . . .*

HD and I arrived in New Haven the same year: I came directly from Philadelphia and she after a sojourn in Europe. Her arrival warranted more press in *The New Haven Register*. When she sat on the stone wall outside Yale's Sterling Library with Norman Holmes Pearson two green miles separated us. At that moment I was tearing down the sidewalk on my red tricycle forming free verse in my head. No cars trundled across High Street, she and Pearson had an unobstructed view of the Cross Campus. The 'shelf' he had promised her at Yale was now a reality.

She had grown in stature since her days in Amherst. As ED she was 5'6" but those young years in Bethlehem jumping stiles had added a full 5" to her height. Still shy and uncomfortable with travel.

After posing for a photograph with Pearson and Bryher, they walked along College Street admiring elms on The Green. At the corner of Chapel Street Bryher and HD said good evening to Pearson and turned into the smoke shop next to the Shubert Theatre for cigarettes. HD wasn't thinking about me as the elevator rose to the top floor of the Taft. The drapes in her suite had been pulled back by the maid. Her rooms looked west. She sat by the window abstractly taking in the cleft of West Rock throwing her shadow up Chapel Street. I overturned my tricycle. While my mother ran cool water over my scraped knee she didn't say "Shush, shush. Lift straight your chin. HD is near."

The moon drifted through the black deciduous, a disc of bright at the ragged hulk of West Rock. HD was above all this. The traffic light at the corner of Chapel and College blinked for no one. My sheets were newly clean, I watched through two pines the traffic light switch, beacons of red and green coming to me. At the corner of Chapel and Central I listened for one car roaring south and the air of a poem entering me. "Their breath was your gift."

# Emily Dickinson's Defunct

MARILYN NELSON

She used to
pack poems
in her hip pocket.
Under all the
gray old lady
clothes she was
dressed for action.
She had hair,
imagine,
in certain places, and
believe me
she smelled human
on a hot summer day.
Stalking snakes
or counting
the thousand motes
in sunlight
she walked just
like an Indian.
She was New England's
favorite daughter,
she could pray
like the devil.
She was a
two-fisted woman,
this babe.
All the flies
just stood around
and buzzed
when she died.

# *Emily* –

PETER NICHOLSON

Now the Bride of poetry beckons
From her brutal sleep
With each part of truth protesting
At mortality.

She was lonelier than our suburbs
Yet as true and living
Though the same chimeras beckoned
With the same leave-taking.

On her Amherst springtime forehead
Set with laurel's fire
She is hymning into being
Dazzled crests of time.

Bird of summer in her hair,
Wing of autumn on her breast,
Wedded to the winter snow
And each joy confessed.

Soldered with transcendences,
In her room a furnace,
Butterfly and bee contriving
Sceptre, crown and chalice.

Now your coronation's given,
Entrance to imperium,
Veiled with stars and continents,
Your brocade delirium,

Each packet stitched and put away,
Ships of Asian spices,
Harboured to desuetude,
Daguerreotype left over.

For once a passion that will last
Past what rusts and buckles,
There with Walt in double grandeur,
Mystery's odd couple.

Rushing to the sunlight's shards,
Toppling to greatness,
Adoration in your nerve
And the bandaged fierceness

We thought closer to our time —
Yours was purer, truer,
With those words that cauterise
The mouthline's wounded murmur.

There is wonder wide enough
To fold all things within it,
Intoxication offered up
With a goodness granted;

Yours — by right of the burden given,
Yours — by the White Election,
Yours — though centuries steal away,
Yet ours, at the end, your perfection.

# Emily in Choir

KATHLEEN NORRIS

Emily holds her father's hand;
she dances in place
through the Invitatory,
and refuses the book with no pictures.
"This is boring," she whispers
in the silence between psalms.

Candles lit in honor of the guardian angels
make rivers of air that bend the stone
walls of the abbey church. "Why are the men
wearing costumes?" Emily asks.
"They're the brothers,"
her father explains, and Emily says, "Well!
They must have a very strict mother!"

*The Grave is strict*, says another Emily;
Emily-here-and-now plays with the three
shadows her hands make
on the open page. *While the clergyman
tells Father and Vinnie that "this Corruptible
shall put on Incorruption," it has already done so
and they go defrauded.*

Brimful of knowledge, Emily shakes my arm:
"They're the monks," she says,
"the men who sing" and she runs
up the aisle, out into the day,
to *where the angels are . . .*

*In the name of the Bee —
And of the Butterfly —
And of the Breeze — Amen!*

Note: "Emily in Choir": An Invitatory is a psalm sung at the beginning of a prayer
service. Quotations are from Emily Dickinson: Poem #408, Letter #508 (1873), and
Poem #18.

# "Half-Cracked Poetess"

JOYCE CAROL OATES


On my finger an antique ring I hadn't
deserved, but got. Like so much, you're thinking
meanly, and you'd be right.
And now the stone is cracked, a tiny disaster,
the opal's mild fiery light stares out
and no reflection.
Like an eye, in a way. Blind
but still seeing
except, what is it seeing? —
and why?

# Emily Dickinson's Writing Table in Her Bedroom at the Homestead, Amherst, Mass.

SHARON OLDS

The chair next to her writing table
is the chair my parents tied me to
that day. Not the same chair,
but a cousin of it,
a Hitchcock from Connecticut,
factory beside sluice gates
through which shad leap, rubefacted
with roe. My cervical vertebra
feels the peneblum. My swayback sways
away from the lower bar, and I can almost
still feel, with my buttocks, the maze
of glazed string in the seat. My wrists
do not remember being tied
to the struts rising from the seat, it makes me
uneasy to try to remember that.
But I remember the alphabet soup she fed me,
the pleasure of being spoon-fed, I wanted
to read each dense message as if it were
falling, intelligible manna. When I was
alone in the room I would drift . . . I had never
been without pencil or paper – no scissors,
no Scotch tape. I would sing, sometimes,
loaf-shaped quatrains from the hymnal, but when someone
approached I'd be silent. When my father came in,
I wonder what it was like for him
to come into a room with his child tied to a chair in it,
I think he liked it, I think it felt
right to him, he had great faith in me.
I would be a chair that grew up
and spoke well and went to his college.
I was the maple they tapped, troughed,
I was their Druid, they trusted me, they
knew if there was to be sweetness ever come
out of that house, it would have to come from me.

# Frowning at Emily

ALICIA SUSKIN OSTRIKER

The entire room was frowning at Emily
They wanted to know if she was crazy or what
It disturbed them she wrote so many poems
About death madness suffering,
Like: a normal person wouldn't do that,
Would they,
But they were too polite to complain, so
I had to make a speech about it.
Said: you know there are two basic
Approaches to life, some of us try to protect ourselves
Hoping no harm will happen to us
We try for damage control
We cover our rear ends don't we
While others want to experience everything
And are prepared to take the
Consequences — I was making this up
And just one kid in the room
Grinned and exclaimed "cool"
Under his breath.
Of course he was the boy
Who'd had four years of Latin
In high school and loved Virgil
But hell, we're grateful for whatever comes,
Aren't we.

# for Emily (Dickinson)

MAUREEN OWEN


The girl    working the xerox in the stationery store
has a "thing"    for one of the customers        "I'm in love!"
she blurts to the complete strangers buying stamp pad ink.
"Am I shaking?                    Last week when he came in            I
stapled my thumb."            It's not just a shift in season
but a hormone that sets the trees off too        from plain
green they go        cheeks flushed                & dropping
everything!
Like the baby bashing through them   hooting                "More!"
&    the radio    announcing        "It's a Sealy Posturepedic morning!"
the landscape's gone silly   with abundance of motif        where
the tossed baby    Plunks      into the damp pyramid        &
is gone            From the base a small scuffed shoe
chanting   "Leafs!    Leafs!"                        Here
is all the drama of the emperor's flight!      Imperial
dragon robes swept up        porcelains scattered
& the eerie glazed stillness    the soft mist Thudding
where the stately picnic        had been.
Is it a theory of numbers                or just        Quantity
that lifts us        up from under the armpits        with Fred
Astaire singing      in grand finale crescendo            "It
doesn't matter where you get it      as long as you got it!"


                        O furious Excesses!
She set her tough skiff        straightway
into the sea        for love of danger!
            tho all the birds have lost   their cover
                    & You        O Bald October
                        I knew you  when you
                        still had hair!

# [*Most sensual of recluses*]

RON PADGETT


Most sensual of recluses, faint
Daughter, surrounded by a haze
Of daguerreotypes, more than

"passing fair;"

I come upon you

in the lines

"At the Cattle Show of 1856, so we are told,
Emily Dickinson gained a second prize with
a loaf of her 'rye and Indian bread.'"

To imagine your nervousness, delicate hands poised among cattle!
And the red ribbon or blue ribbon against your black dress;
Did you even let escape from out the corner of your mouth
A bird? Did your father drop a word upon the space between
Your front teeth?

(In mid-afternoon I see a taut, thin
string of tannish color stretched
between a second story window and
the hands of some idiot child? I am
a jealous lover, must know what was
in that basket!)

And who is this elderly man who delivers letters in his hat?
You gained only a second prize and I am glad.

It is said
you spoke to nervous guests, seated in the parlor, from
the hall, through, perhaps, a skeined curtain; and further,
were hesitant to address letters in your own hand . . .

# Emily Dickinson

LINDA PASTAN

We think of her hidden in a white dress
among the folded linens and sachets
of well kept cupboards, or just out of sight
sending jellies and notes with no address
to all the wondering Amherst neighbors.
Eccentric as New England weather
the stiff wind of her mind, stinging or gentle,
blew two half imagined lovers off.
Yet legend won't explain the sheer sanity
of vision, the serious mischief
of language, the economy of pain.

# Because I Could Not Dump

ANDREA PATERSON

Because I could not Dump the Trash —
Joe kindly stopped for Me —
The Garbage Truck held but Ourselves —
And Bacterial Colonies —

We slowly drove — Joe smelled of Skunk —
Yet risking no delay
My hairdo and composure too,
Were quickly Fumed away —

We passed a School, where Dumpsters stood
Recycling — in the Rain —
We picked up Yields of Industry —
Dead Cats and Window Panes —

Or rather — Joe picked up —
Seeing maggot-lined cans — I recoiled —
When heir to smelly Legacies,
What sort of Woman — Spoils?

We paused before a Dump that seemed
A Swelling of the Ground —
The Soil was scarcely visible —
Joe dropped — his Booty — down.

Since then — 'tis a fortnight — yet
Seems shorter than the Day
I first set out the Old Fish Heads —
And hoped Joe'd come my Way —

# Desire

MOLLY PEACOCK

It doesn't speak and it isn't schooled,
like a small foetal animal with wettened fur.
It is the blind instinct for life unruled,
visceral frankincense and animal myrrh.
It is what babies bring to kings,
an eyes-shut, ears-shut medicine of the heart
that smells and touches endings and beginnings
without the details of time's experienced part-
fit-into-part-fit-into-part. Like a paw,
it is blunt; like a pet who knows you
and nudges your knee with its snout – but more raw
and blinder and younger and more divine, too,
than the tamed wild – it's the drive for what is real,
deeper than the brain's detail: the drive to feel.

# Feathered Friends

ROBERT PETERS

A splendid Fellow in the Grass
Occasionally rides —
I know you've seen him — did you not
His clucking noisy is —

The Grass divides as with a Comb —
His glossy Feathers quaver —
He beaks his Biddy's little Comb
And shoves it to her Liver —

He likes her secret Parts —
They are so sweet and soupy —
And when he's through and doth withdraw —
His tiny Shaft is juicy —

Most of Nature's feathered Friends
I know, and they know me —
I feel for them a transport —
Of erotic Cordiality —

Except for this randy Fellow —
Old Chanticleer the Bold —
He leaves me tighter breathing —
And quivering with Cold.

# Emily Dickinson's Ankle

JOHN REINHARD

Shitfaced at deer camp
we sit and toast to
eight-point bucks, to
too much red wine
in the venison gravy, to
the cool and lengthening nights
of autumn, to Emily Dickinson's
white dress, to the old farmwomen
of Nebraska who've turned to
poetry, to the way
love hangs from the human form
like silk and finally
to the human form itself when
Buck Lund offers up his glass
saying, "Here's to a woman's feet,
to the ankle and arch
and the way the foot moves
even when she's standing still,"
and Kent swirls his wine,
"Jesus, yes, there's nothing
more underrated, sexier,
than a woman's foot";
since these guys are hunters
maybe they fall in love
with what leaves tracks
in the snow and lets them
follow, and then Jane says,
"Men like whatever body
part they can get to
with the least difficulty —
this is not a matter
of aesthetics," Jane says.
so everyone looks at me,
waits, until I respond,
shitfaced at deer camp,
"I like a woman's smile,"

and the men groan and Buck
says, "You're growing soft,
old buddy. A smile? More
than breasts heavy with milk
or air or whatever
breasts get heavy with?
More than ankles? Red-tipped
toes?" and I have to admit
I almost said, "A nice fanny"
and thought of some
I followed for a while, yet
I never fell in love with someone
because I liked walking
behind her, while I've chased
women whose smiles
excited me, teased me close
toward something
genuine, broad, bottomless
as desire, and Jane says,
"I like the smile, too;
besides, have you ever seen
a man with nice feet?" Soon
all the bodies, shitfaced
at deer camp, give way
to sleep and forgiveness
and the various boundaries
of our delight.

In the morning's fresh light
the stags will bound
toward sky and some will not come down
as men pretend themselves
to leaves and burst
with fire, while I,
no gunman, keep long as I can
to my night's dream, this time
of Emily Dickinson, who leads me
to a small room
where she reads a poem
I've not heard before

of death and life in one
breath, and there
I throw myself at Emily's feet,
at an ankle
alone and too long sad
where I kiss her round moment
of bone, its poetry, her small
alabaster moon, and how
it shines, how it smiles,
how in light steps it gives
shape to one more
distant, tideless
landscape.

# Emily Dickinson's Mirror, Amherst

DONALD REVELL

Its flecked surface a map of disappearing islands,
the glass imposes a narrowing, flat sense
of time and limited space upon the room
at all angles. Looking into it head on,
I feel contained and ready to understand
the short lines' skewed New England syntax mouthed
into so strict a frame. A discipline
of words arrayed for the bridal and no groom
wanted. In each of us, there must be one
oracular, strait emptiness a hand's
breadth across that is ourselves in proud
fear, looking into our own eyes for doctrine
and the one audience whose accents we can
share wholly. The purist's God. Pride's mirror and island.

# "I Am in Danger—Sir—"

ADRIENNE RICH

"Half-cracked" to Higginson, living,
afterward famous in garbled versions,
your hoard of dazzling scraps a battlefield,
now your old snood

mothballed at Harvard
and you in your variorum monument
equivocal to the end —
who are you?

Gardening the day-lily,
wiping the wine-glass stems,
your thought pulsed on behind
a forehead battered paper-thin,

you, woman, masculine
in single-mindedness,
for whom the word was more
than a symptom —

a condition of being.
Till the air buzzing with spoiled language
sang in your ears
of Perjury

and in your half-cracked way you chose
silence for entertainment,
chose to have it out at last
on your own premises.

# The Houses of Emily Dickinson

LARRY RUBIN

It is, of course, the wrong house.
The one next door seems much more likely
To have sheltered an aging spinster
Rattling her chains in the garret
Or burning through beds with puritan heat.
Emily – and Charlotte – are names for the moors,
For Victorian gables and turrets, gothic stairs;
But our Emily dwelt in a brick house
Suitable for a sorority in Charlottesville,
Nor are there seven gables in this solid residence
Of the Amherst treasurer.
Still, daughters with a literary bent
Can do funny things with their father's land.
They can take a tree, or a robin,
Or a garden,
And fiddle with it till its roots are screwed
Into the earth of words to such a depth
That dirt meets sky, and alabaster
Is the mode for every chamber –
Whether the structure be brick or frame.
She has pierced this heavy parasol with light;
All houses, for her, it seems, are right.

# The Upper Story

MARY JO SALTER

As Emily Dickinson
would not come down, I'm
sorry, but I've felt the need to climb
the worn steps to her room,
winding up the stair
as if into her inner ear.

*Art*, as she once said,
*is a House that tries to be haunted*,
and as I stand
on the landing where she curled in shadow
to listen to the piano
and soprano voice of Mabel Todd

(her editor years later —
who now graciously accepted
a poem and glass of sherry in place
of having seen her face),
this would become that House.
No trespass can erase

what she once made of it —
the gate she opened, resolute
to escape, and just as quickly shut:
*I think I was held in check by some
invisible agent* . . . And when she wrote
*Again — his voice is at the door —*

here is the door she meant.
Her room, probably Spartan
even when lived in, now holds but few
fabled artifacts: a snow-white
coverlet; a "sleigh bed," narrow
like a wooden shoe; a snipped

lily of a dress, limp in the closet;
a wilted hatbox; a woven basket
she'd lower, something like Rapunzel,
full of gingerbread.
Or so our guide has said. Yet
devoted to the genuine

as she was — first jasmine of the season,
hummingbird and snake —
I doubt she would have taken umbrage
when learned men in Cambridge
spirited off her writing table
to higher education. A double

(its surface little more
than two feet square, and where
poems commensurately small
were scrawled on backs of envelopes)
sits convincingly beneath the tall
window onto Main Street.

*To shut our eyes is Travel,*
and that table may as well
be anywhere as here.
She'd have held close whatever house
she was born in, as a squirrel
clutches its acorn; but with a need

not wholly fed by fear.
At twenty-four, moving back
to her birthplace, she'd lived the thought
transposed: To travel, shut the eyes.
*I supposed we were going to make a "transit,"*
*as heavenly bodies did . . .*

She was truly half-
astonished at those carriages
and cartons — almost as if
she'd lived only in that other life,

unseen, in her upper story.
*Touch Shakespeare for me,*

she wrote to Mabel in Europe,
thinking her close enough.
Why had anyone expressed the hope
to see Emily, who'd compare in letters
her unmet friends to Peter's
Christ: "whom having not seen, ye love"?

Finding nothing and no time
impalpable, she'd call
attention to the Biblical
"house not made with hands" for all
who'd listen. Wasn't that her home
as much as this was? Fame,

a lower form of Immortality,
in the intervening century
has unpacked her cradle to restore
its place, steps from her deathbed.
*There is no first, or last, in Forever . . .*
To the West, across the field

from another window, lives the family
at The Evergreens, whom Emily
saw little more than I can: Austin
and dark sister-in-law Sue.
*I would have come out of Eden*
*to open the Door for you . . .*

but she hadn't had to.
Drumming down the stair,
my ears fill with the spirals of a fly
a poem let in and won't be shown the way:
as if that buzzing, when she died,
were here still amplified.

# Emily Dickinson

GARY SMITH

I've defended you against the many
who have made a madcap of you –
citing the middle years, how feverishly
you paced the house in bridal whites,
the longing of every poem you wrote –
how easily they spill into nothing.
We like to own the poets we keep –
to mother each word like obsessions.
Your company is not easily kept –
too soon, too soon you retire to bed.
A peevish old maid worrying Puritans.
If heaven had been given to you in gold,
before singing your hymns of praise,
you would have discovered copper within.

# Emily Dickinson Reading Walt Whitman

BARTON LEVI ST. ARMAND

I heard he was disgraceful, and he is!
The bearded rapist lurking in these folds
of velvet mossy-green, the Gift Book's gilt –
so innocent, so flowery, so genteel!
How could Father guess? No doubt he thinks
it is some girlish album full of gush
bought by his cast-iron railroad stock
(a stripèd adder nestling in the pile
of books he buys and begs me not to read).
What would Father do? He sits in state
below, assured the pious pages of
the *Sabbath Visitor* have nothing carnal in them
(dry as starched papyrus in the tomb),
while Emily receives a private caller.
*"I mind how we lay in June, such a*
                    *transparent summer morning;*
*You settled your head athwart my hips and gently*
                    *turned over upon me.*
*And parted the shirt from my bosom-bone, and plunged your*
                    *tongue to my barestript heart . . ."*
Did Father feel like this when sanctified?
Signed, sealed, delivered by Christ's blizzard-kiss
to title in the company of Saints?
*"These are the thoughts of all men in all ages . . .*
*They are not original with me . . ."*
My hands grow stiff as death; physically I feel
as if the top of my head were taken off;
in spite of the squat air-tight's patent heat,
I turn so cold no fire can ever warm me.
Can this be poetry, or is it God
come for me as Father said he would?
*"I am not an earth nor an adjunct of an earth,*
*I am the mate and companion of all people, all*
                    *just as immortal and fathomless as myself;*
*They do not know how immortal, but I know . . ."*
If this be "poison," then I down my dram!

"*Who need be afraid of the merge?*
*Undrape. . . . you are not guilty to me, nor stale nor discarded,*
*I see through the broadcloth and gingham whether or no,*
*And am around, tenacious, acquisitive, tireless . . . and*
                        *can never be shaken away . . ."*
What rosy fingers nibble at my gown?
"*. . . voices veiled, and I remove the veil . . ."*
                \   \   \
The picket gate goes "*chunk*," and latches shut.
                \   \   \
Not my veil. No, that remains untouched;
inviolate, invisible, unassumed —
This *camerado* shall not penetrate
where sister, brother, lover drown alone
and even dread Jehovah skulks away,
cheated of the final nudity.
A poker stirs the white ash of the coals
as I consign these *Leaves* to leaves of flame,
without the Quaker poet's righteous wrath
(poor Whittier could not believe his eyes!).

"*I depart as air . . . I effuse my flesh in eddies and*
                        *drift it in lacy jags . . ."*
My web is cleansed. Dear Father will not know
the heathen suttee blazing in his house
destroying and preserving for that once
which is Eternity.
                Now I can write
again to Mr. Higginson who said
of Mr. Whitman it was no discredit
that he wrote his book but only that
he did not take and burn it afterwards.

# Emily

WILLIAM STAFFORD

On that page where the whole world moved
and other people ran
frantic in their lives to stay the same,
she was the stillest one –

Eye in the night to lag or surge,
ready to catch the shine
of the newest star or the old sky in the brain
where the right word again begins time.

# Lithograph of Amherst

LYNN STRONGIN

*Agony enacted there*
*Motionless as peace*
*— Emily Dickinson*

The calm ribbon of air
  is
a lost language lesson.

Towns
  like etchings under glass
resemble this one.

Day's profile
  is arrested
arrogant, precise.

Footprints
  are covered
by leaves & ice.

Time irons
  pressmarks
& bubbles in.

Color is borne home
  the hue of birds' wings
the hue of old bone.

           *    *    *

Fate stopped
  at this desk, this town:
The shining black inkwell. Then moved on.

# Lost and Found

MARK VINZ

*Some keep the sabbath going to*
    *church;*
*I keep it staying at home.*
*— Emily Dickinson*


Sunday morning, blues on the radio —
I know that tune too well,
buried in my chair with football scores
while all the family sleeps.
What's lost is found and lost again,
the Sunday morning paradox —
between the then and now,
the stop and start again,
a church bell and a mouth harp toll.

I sit with news I didn't want to read —
threats of war and promises no one will keep.
Furnace surges, snowflakes gather
on the window sill, a jet plane rattles glass,
and all the house is fast asleep.

# Between the Lines

THEODORE WEISS

You, alive, seldom put yourself
on view. Was it that you knew
the outrageous light shuttered away
in you, confronted directly, stark
when most elate, must shrivel
its beholder?
     Unwary latecomers,
dead set on finding you out,
pry into your lines.
      And yet
I doubt you would object. Instead,
you — a star that's left and left
its light, grown stronger, gathering
as it travels, as it has the space
of dark and time to swell out in,
and also those asquint to read you
by your radiance — would dazzle.

Your words, wide awake, enticing,
flit away before their hands
can touch.
    And still they feel
the fragrant wind those words are
fanning, feel the shadows wading by
of greater (being so elusive) light.

But you will never give them
what they want and so they want
it more. This way they're almost
satisfied. You too who long ago
discovered how to live, enormously,
containedly, between the lines.

# Altitudes

RICHARD WILBUR

1

    Look up into the dome:
It is a great salon, a brilliant place,
    Yet not too splendid for the race
Whom we imagine there, wholly at home

    With the gold-rosetted white
Wainscot, the oval windows, and the fault-
    Less figures of the painted vault.
Strolling, conversing in that precious light,

    They chat no doubt of love,
The pleasant burden of their courtesy
    Borne down at times to you and me
Where, in this dark, we stand and gaze above.

    For all they cannot share,
All that the world cannot in fact afford,
    Their lofty premises are floored
With the massed voices of continual prayer.

2

    How far it is from here
To Emily Dickinson's father's house in America;
    Think of her climbing a spiral stair
Up to the little cupola with its clear

    Small panes, its room for one.
Like the dark house below, so full of eyes
    In mirrors and of shut-in flies,
This chamber furnished only with the sun

Is she and she alone,
A mood to which she rises, in which she sees
    Bird-choristers in all the trees
And a wild shining of the pure unknown

    On Amherst. This is caught
In the dormers of a neighbor, who, no doubt,
    Will before long be coming out
To pace about his garden, lost in thought.

# To Dickinson

DIANE WILLIAMS

SERIOUSLY AND POLITELY I tell the story to persons of the loss of you.

It was good to see you.     It was really good to see you. Oh, you are lucky.

If the pleasant world contains, as we hope it does, anything of lasting value, which was once mine, I believe you have it.

In anger, therefore, in anger, I send documents in the midst of this ritual as I tell the story of the loss of you. This is the delayed discovery of you somewhere mysterious here in New York City, then the disappearance of you again and again! – is it that you do not approve of me? That's what I think.

I will not say anything bad about your rebellion. Your unceasing progress, your reforms, your improvements of every kind, in every way – you may be the best person who has ever lived.

# To Emily Dickinson

YVOR WINTERS

Dear Emily, my tears would burn your page,
But for the fire-dry line that makes them burn —
Burning my eyes, my fingers, while I turn
Singly the words that crease my heart with age.
If I could make some tortured pilgrimage
Through words or Time or the blank pain of Doom
And kneel before you as you found your tomb,
Then I might rise to face my heritage.

Yours was an empty upland solitude
Bleached to the powder of a dying name;
The mind, lost in a word's lost certitude
That faded as the fading footsteps came
To trace an epilogue to words grown odd
In that hard argument which led to God.

# Emily Dickinson at Coleville

HAROLD WITT

We never know how high we are, I said
in Coleville's night – till we are called to rise.
I couldn't sleep. I'd left my barrack bed
and gone out under star-pulsating skies.
My stature tried to touch them as I sat;
the bluish snowy mountains glimmered and gleamed.
I didn't even light a cigarette.
I could be true to plan, it almost seemed.
I sighed. I hardly feared to be a king –
not much chance of that, but in that air
heroism was a daily thing,
or would be, Emily said – and did I dare?
I sat there quoting her on a rocky slope,
hoping my heightened cubits wouldn't warp.

# Visiting Emily Dickinson

CHARLES WRIGHT

We stood in the cupola for a while,
                                JT, Joe Langland and I,
And then they left and I sat
Where she'd sat, and looked through the oak tree toward the hat factory
And down to the river, the railroad

Still there, the streets where the caissons growled
                                        with their blue meat
Still there, and Austin and Sue's still there
Next door on the other side.
And the train station at the top of the hill.
                                And I sat there and I sat there

A decade or so ago
One afternoon toward the end of winter, the oak tree
Floating its ganglia like a dark cloud
                                outside the window.
Or like a medusa hung up to dry.

And nothing came up through my feet like electric fire.
And no one appeared in a white dress
                                with white flowers
Clutched in her white, tiny hands:
No voice from nowhere said anything
                                about living and dying in 1862.

But I liked it there. I liked
The way sunlight lay like a shirtwaist over the window seat.
I liked the view down to the garden.
                                I liked the boxwood and evergreens.
And the wren-like, sherry-eyed figure

I kept thinking I saw there
                as the skies started to blossom
And a noiseless noise began to come from the orchard —
And I sat very still, and listened hard
And thought I heard it again.
                And then there was nothing, nothing at all.

The slick bodice of sunlight
                smoothed out on the floorboards,
The crystal I'd turned inside of
Dissembling to shine and a glaze somewhere near the windowpanes,
Voices starting to drift up from downstairs,
                somebody calling my name . . .

# Emily Dickinson, Bismarck and the Roadrunner's Inquiry

RAY YOUNG BEAR

I never thought for a moment
that it was simply an act of fondness
which prompted me to compose
and send these letters.
Surely into each I held
the same affection as when
we were together on a canoe
over Lake Agassiz in Manitoba,
paddling toward a moonlit fog
before we lost each other.

From this separation came
the Kingfisher, whose blue and white
colored bands on chest and neck
represent the lake-water and the fog.
But this insignia also stands
for permafrost and aridity:
two climate conditions
I could not live in.

It's necessary to keep your apparition
a secret: your bare shoulders,
your ruffled blouse, and the smooth
sounds of the violin you play
are the things which account
for this encomium for the Algonquin-
speaking goddess of beauty.

Like the caterpillar's toxin
that discourages predators,
I am accustomed to food
which protects me,
camouflages me.
I would be out of place
in the tundra or desert,

hunting moose for its meat and hide,
tracking roadrunners for their feathers.

But our dialects are nearly the same!
Our Creation stories begin on a neat
floor of undigested bones,
overlooking the monolithic glaciers.
This is what we are supposed to have
seen before our interglacial internment.
That time before the Missouri River
knew where to go.

My memory starts under the earth
where the Star-Descendant taught me
to place hot coals on my forearm.
"In the afterlife, the scar tissue
will emit the glow of a firefly,
enabling one to expedite the rebirth
process. This light guides one's way
from Darkness."

The day I heard from you,
I accidentally fell down the steps
of a steamboat and lost consciousness,
which was befitting because
there was little rationale
for the play (I had just watched
onboard) of a man who kept
trying to roll a stone uphill,
a stone which wanted to roll downhill.
I found myself whispering
"No business politicizing myth"
the moment I woke up.
Gradually, in the form of blood
words began to spill from
my injuries: Eagle feathers
1 — 2 — 3 & 4 on Pipestone.

I now keep vigil for silhouettes
of boats disappearing over
the arête horizon.

I keep seeing our correspondence
arrange itself chronologically,
only to set itself ablaze,
and the smoke turns to radiant
but stationary cloud-islands,
suspended on strings above

Mt. St. Helens, Mt. Hood
and Mt. Shasta: Three Sisters
waiting Joseph's signal.
They tell me of your dissatisfaction
in my society where traffic signs
overshadow the philosophy
of being Insignificant.
It is no different
than living under a bridge in Texas
beside the Rio Grande.
Please accept advice from the Blind
pigmentless Salamander
who considers his past an inurement.
"Perplexity should be expected,
especially when such a voyage
is imminent."

I want to keep you as the year
I first saw your tainted photograph,
preserved in an oval wooden frame
with thick convex glass,
opposite the introvert
you were supposed to be,
walking in from the rain,
a swan minus the rheumatism.

All of a sudden it is difficult
to draw and paint your face
with graphic clarity,
when the initial response is to alter
your age.
Automatically, the bright colors
of Chagall replace the intent.

When the Whirlwind returned
as a constellation,
we asked for cultural acquittance,
but when the reply appeared as herons

skimming along the updraft
of the Reservation's ridge,
we asked again.
It was never appropriate.
We were disillusioned,
and our request became immune
to illness, misfortune and plain hate,
or so we thought.

Contempt must have predetermined
our destiny.
To no avail I have attempted to
reconstruct the drifting halves
to side with me.
All that time and great waste.
Positive moon, negative sun.

Way before she began to blossom
into a flower capable of destroying
or healing, and even during the times
she precariously engaged herself
to different visions,
I was already dependent upon her.
Whenever we were fortunate
to appear within each other's prisms,
studying and imploring our emissaries
beyond the stations
of our permanence,
I had no words to offer.

Mesmerized, she can only regret
and conform to the consequences
of an inebriate's rage
while I recede from her
a listless river

who would be glad
to cleanse and touch
the scar the third mutant-flower
made as it now burns and flourishes
in her arms.

I would go ahead and do this
without hint or indication
you would accept me,
Dear Emily.

Jean Balderston is a psychotherapist who lives and works in New York City. Her love of Emily Dickinson began when she pulled from a childhood Christmas stocking a packet of bookplates inscribed "There is no frigate like a Book / To take us Lands away." Her doctoral dissertation is a study of the poet's family, *The Edward Dickinsons of Amherst — A Family Analysis.*

Marvin Bell lives in Iowa City, Iowa; Sag Harbor, New York; and Port Townsend, Washington. Among his sixteen collections of poems are *The Book of the Dead Man, Ardor,* and an enlarged edition of *Selected Poems.*

John Berryman received the Pulitzer Prize for *77 Dream Songs* in 1967. At the time of his death in 1972 at the age of fifty-seven, the number of dream songs grew to 385. Among his collections of poetry are *Homage to Mistress Bradstreet* (1956), *Berryman's Sonnets* (1967), *Henry's Fate* (1977), and *Collected Poems: 1937–1971.*

Robert Bly's many books of poems include *Silence in the Snowy Fields, The Light Around the Body,* winner of the National Book Award, and most recently *Eating the Honey of Words: New and Selected Poems.* His essays have been collected in *Iron John, The Sibling Society, The Maiden King* (with Marion Woodman), and *American Poetry: Wildness and Domesticity.*

Marianne Boruch has published four collections of poetry, *View from the Gazebo* (1983), and *Descendant* (1989), *Moss Burning* (1993), and *A Stick that Breaks and Breaks* (1997), as well as a book of essays, *Poetry's Old Air.* She teaches in Purdue University's MFA program.

Lucie Brock-Broido is the author of two collections of poetry, *A Hunger* and *The Master Letters,* both from Knopf. She is director of poetry in the School of Arts at Columbia University and lives in New York City and in Cambridge, Massachusetts.

Jayne Relaford Brown received her MFA in creative writing from San Diego State University. She writes and teaches composition in Reading, Pennsylvania.

Andrea Carlisle is the author of *The Riverhouse Stories,* winner of the Oregon Coast Council for the Arts Award. She lives in Portland, Oregon. For many years, she taught both fiction and nonfiction at Clark College, the Oregon Writers' Workshop, Oregon Writers' Colony, and Portland State University.

Siv Cedering is the author of eighteen books, including two novels, six books for children, and several collections of poetry, including *Letters from the Floating World* and most recently *Letters from an Observatory: New and Selected Poems 1973–1998.* Also a painter and sculptor, she lives on Long Island in New York.

Amy Clampitt was born in Providence, Iowa, in 1920. She published her first poem in *The New Yorker* in 1978. Her first full-length collection, *The Kingfisher*, was published at the age of sixty-three. Her collections of poems include *What the Light was Like* (1985), *Archaic Figure* (1987), *Westward* (1990), and *A Silence Opens* (1994). *The Collected Poems of Amy Clampitt* was published in 1997. She worked as a freelance editor, a reference librarian at the Audubon Society, and as a secretary at the Oxford University Press. Later in her life, she taught at the College of William and Mary and Smith College. She died in 1994.

Sheila Coghill is professor of English and a former chair of the Department of English at Minnesota State University Moorhead, where she specializes in American Literature and teaches a senior capstone seminar in Whitman and Dickinson. She has studied at the Jung Institute in Zurich, Switzerland, and is currently finishing a book-length study of Emily Dickinson and alchemy.

Billy Collins is the author of several books of poetry, most recently *Picnic, Lightning*.

Martha Collins is the author of four books of poems, the most recent of which is *Some Things Words Can Do* in 1998. She has also cotranslated, with the author, *The Women Carry River Water*, a collection of poems by the Vietnamese poet Nguyen Quang Thieu. She is codirector of the creative writing program at Oberlin College, where she serves as editor of *Field* magazine.

Hart Crane's "To Dickinson," composed in 1926 and published in 1927, is one of the earliest poems to recognize Dickinson's work as influential and pivotal in American literature. Crane was born in Garrettsville, Ohio, in 1899. Considered by many to be among the first visionary modernists, Crane is the author of two major collections of poems, *White Buildings* and the important and influential book-length poem, *The Bridge* (1930). On his return to the United States from Mexico where he had been living in 1927, Crane committed suicide by jumping from the ship carrying him back to New York. *The Complete Poems and Selected Letters and Prose* was published in 1966.

Philip Dacey's most recent books, his sixth and seventh, are *The Deathbed Playboy* and *The Paramour of the Moving Air*. His latest chapbook is *What's Empty Weighs the Most: 24 Sonnets*.

Madeline DeFrees's most recent of six collections of poetry is *Possible Sibyls*. A commemorative chapbook titled *Double Dutch* was published in 1999. She has held a National Endowment for the Arts grant and Guggenheim Fellowship in poetry. She resides in Seattle, Washington.

Toi Derricotte is the author of *Tender*, a collection of poems, and *The Black Notebooks: An Interior Journey* (1997), a prose memoir. She currently lives in Pittsburgh, Pennsylvania, where she teaches in the MFA in writing program at the University of Pittsburgh.

Richard Eberhart's many collections of poems include *New and Selected Poems,*

*1930–1990, Maine Poems* and *Collected Poems: 1930–1986.* In 1966 he received the Pulitzer Prize for his *Selected Poems: 1930–1965.*

Lynn Emanuel was born in New York and has lived, worked, and traveled in North Africa, Europe, and the Near East. She is the author of three books of poetry, *Hotel Fiesta, The Dig,* and *Then, Suddenly.* Currently, she is a professor of English at the University of Pittsburgh and director of the writing program.

Dave Etter is the author of more than fifteen collections of poems, including *Selected Poems* (1987), *Sunflower County* (1994), *How High the Moon* (1996), and, most recently, *Next Time You See Me.* He lives in Lanark, Illinois.

Annie Finch's collection of poetry *Eve* appeared in 1997. She has just completed translating *The Complete Poems of Louise Labe,* a woman poet of the French Renaissance. She is also author of a book on poetics, *The Ghost of Meter: Culture and Prosody: American Free Verse* and editor of several anthologies including *A Formal Feeling Comes: Poems in Form by Contemporary Women.*

Richard Foerster is the author of three collections of poetry: *Sudden Harbor* (1992), *Patterns of Descent* (1993), and *Trillium,* which received Honorable Mention for the 2000 Poets' Prize. A new collection, *Cutting Losses,* will be published in 2001. A staff member of the New York–based literary magazine *Chelsea* since 1978, he became its editor in 1994.

Robert Francis was born in Pennsylvania, was educated at Harvard, and spent most of his life living and writing in Amherst, Massachusetts, where he was fond of giving walking tours of Dickinson's house and gravesite to visiting writers. Among his many collections of poems are *The Orb Weaver, Come Out into the Sun: Poems New and Selected,* and *Late Fire, Late Snow: New and Uncollected Poems. Pot Shots at Poetry,* a collection of his essays and criticism, was published in 1980. He died in Amherst in 1987.

Alice Friman, born in New York City, has lived in Indianapolis since 1960. Her collections of poetry include *Reporting from Corinth, Inverted Fire,* and most recently *Zoo,* winner of the 1998 Ezra Pound Poetry Award. She is professor emerita of English and creative writing at the University of Indianapolis.

Alice Fulton's books of poems include: *Sensual Math, Powers of Congress, Palladium,* and *Dance Script with Electric Ballerina.* A collection of essays, *Feeling as a Foreign Language: The Good Strangeness of Poetry* was published in 1999.

Sandra Gilbert, poet, critic, and scholar, is the author of several collections of poems, including *Ghost Volcano Poems, Emily's Bread,* and *In the Fourth World.* Her collections of scholarship and criticism include *No Man's Land: The Place of the Woman Writer in the Twentieth Century, Letters from the Field, Shakespeare's Sisters: Feminist Essays on Women Poets,* and *The Mad Woman in the Attic: A Study of Women and the Literary Imagination of the Nineteenth Century. Wrongful Death: A Memoir,* appeared in 1992. She teaches at the University of California at Davis.

Barry Goldensohn is the author of *St. Venus Eye, Uncarving the Block, The Marrango,* and two chapbooks, *Dance Music* and *East London Pond* (with his wife, Lorrie Goldensohn). He is a professor of English and director of creative writing at Skidmore College.

David Graham is the author of four collections of poems, including *Accidental Blessings, Second Wind,* and *Magic Shows.* He teaches writing and literature at Ripon College in Ripon, Wisconsin. His essay, "The Table Within: Notes on Emily Dickinson," appeared in the *Emily Dickinson International Society Bulletin* in 1997.

Rachel Hadas, poet, translator, and critic, lives in New York and teaches at Rutgers University. She is the author of several collections of poems, including *Pass it On, Mirrors of Astonishment, Empty Bed,* and, most recently, *Halfway Down the Hall: New and Selected Poems.*

Donald Hall is the prolific author of children's books, writing textbooks, and twelve collections of poetry, including, most recently, *Without.* His many books of prose include *String Too Short to be Saved, Their Ancient Glittering Eyes: Remembering Poets and More Poets,* and *Seasons at Eagle Pond.* He lives in the old family farmhouse in New Hampshire.

Lola Haskins has published six collections of poetry, most recently *Extranjera* (1998). Story Line also reissued *Hunger,* which won the Iowa Poetry Prize in 1992, and will publish *Desire Lines: New and Selected Poems,* in fall 2000. She teaches computer science at the University of Florida and lives on a farm outside Gainesville.

William Heyen is professor of English and poet in residence at SUNY Brockport, his undergraduate alma mater. His books of poetry include *Long Island Light; Erika: Poems of the Holocaust; Pterodactyl Rose: Poems of Ecology; The Host: Selected Poems 1965–1990; Diana, Charles, & the Queen,* and *Crazy Horse in Stillness,* winner of the 1997 Small Press Book Award for Poetry. *Pig Notes & Dumb Music: Prose on Poetry,* a *Publisher's Weekly* starred book, appeared in 1998.

Edward Hirsch has published five books of poems, most recently *Earthly Measures* (1994) and *On Love* (1998), and two prose books: *Responsive Reading* (1998) and *How To Read a Poem and Fall in Love with Poetry* (1998). He is a 1998 MacArthur Fellow and teaches in the creative writing program at the University of Houston.

Patricia Y. Ikeda's poetry has appeared most recently in *Premonitions: The Kaya Anthology of New Asian North American Poetry* and *What Book!?: Buddha Poems from Beat to Hiphop.* She writes a column on family life and Buddhist practice for *Turning Wheel,* the journal of the Buddhist Peace Fellowship, and lives with her husband and son in Oakland, California.

Shirley Kaufman has recently edited *Defiant Muse: Hebrew Feminist Poetry from Antiquity to the Present.* She is also the author of *Roots in the Air: New and Selected Poems* and *Gold Country.* She lives in Jerusalem.

X. J. Kennedy has written collections of verse including *Emily Dickinson in*

*Southern California* and *Dark Horses*, several college textbooks, and fourteen books for children. A former English professor, he lives in Lexington, Massachusetts.

Galway Kinnell, a former MacArthur Fellow and State Poet of Vermont, is the author of twelve collections of poetry, including *Selected Poems*, winner of the Pulitzer Prize in 1982 and the American Book Award. His most recent collections are *Imperfect Thirst* (1994) and *A New Selected Poems* (2000). He lives in New York City and Vermont.

Tom Koontz lives in Selma, Indiana, and directs the creative writing program at Ball State University in Muncie, Indiana. He is the editor of The Barnwood Press and *Barnwood*, a poetry magazine. His two recent chapbooks are *In Such a Light* and *Rice Paper Sky*.

Maxine Kumin is the author of more than a dozen collections of poetry, twenty books for children, four novels, and three collections of essays including *Up Country: Poems of New England*, which won the Pulitzer Prize in 1973, *To Make a Prairie*, and *Inside the Halo and Beyond* in 1998. She lives in New Hampshire.

Barbara F. Lefcowitz has published a novel and several books of poetry, most recently *A Hand of Stars*. Also a visual artist, she lives in Bethesda, Maryland.

Lyn Lifshin is the author of numerous collections of poems, most recently *Cold Comfort: Selected Poems* (1997) and *Before It's Light* (1999), both from Black Sparrow Press. She has also edited four anthologies of women's writings, including *Tangled Vines*, *Ariadne's Thread*, and *Lips Unsealed*. An award-winning documentary film of her life and work is entitled *Lyn Lifshin, Not Made of Glass*. She lives in Virginia.

Michael Longley was born in Belfast, Ireland, and educated at the Royal Belfast Academical Institution and Trinity College, Dublin. Among his many collections of poems are *The Echo Gate* (1979), *Selected Poems* (1981), *Poems 1963–1983* (1985), *Gorse Fire* (1991), winner of the Whitbread Prize for Poetry in 1991, *The Ghost Orchid* (1996), *Selected Poems* (1999), and *The Weather in Japan* (2000).

Lee McCarthy lives in Bakersfield, California. Her *Desire's Door* and *Combing Hair with a Seashell* were published in the early nineties. Her *Resistance Every Day of My Life* is forthcoming.

Medbh McGuckian was born in Belfast, Ireland, where she now lives. Her volumes of poetry include *The Flower Master* (1982), *Marconi's Cottage* (1992), *Captain Lavendar* (1995), *Selected Poems* (1997), and *Shelmalier* (1998). She was the first woman to be named writer in residence at Queen's College, Belfast.

Archibald MacLeish was born in 1892. During the 1920s, he published four books of poetry, including *The Happy Marriage* (1924) and *The Poet of Earth* (1925). MacLeish won the Pulitzer Prize for his historical narrative poem "Conquistador" in 1932. In 1949 MacLeish became Harvard's Boylston Professor of Rhetoric and Oratory, a position he held until 1962. From 1963 to 1967 he was Simpson Lecturer at Amherst College. MacLeish continued to write poetry, criticism, and stage- and screenplays, to great acclaim. His *Collected Poems* (1952) won him a second Pulitzer Prize, as well as the National Book Award and the Bollingen Prize. *J.B.* (1958), a verse play based on the book of Job, earned him a third Pulitzer, this time for drama. He died in 1982 in Boston, Massachusetts.

Jay Meek is the author of six collections of poetry, most recently *Headlands: New and Selected Poems*. A former Guggenheim Fellow, he has taught creative writing at MIT, Sarah Lawrence College, Memorial University of Newfoundland, and Wichita State University. He is professor of English and creative writing at the University of North Dakota, where he is poetry editor of the *North Dakota Quarterly*.

Peter Meinke was born in Brooklyn, New York, in 1932. He has published ten books of poetry as well as fiction, criticism, and children's verse. He directed the writing workshop at Eckerd College for twenty-seven years, retiring in 1993. Since then he has been writer in residence at the University of Hawaii (1993), Austin Peay State University in Tennessee, and the University of North Carolina at Greensboro (1996). He lives in St. Petersburg, Florida, with his wife, the artist Jeanne Clark.

Bruce Meyer is founder and director of Canada's largest creative writing program at the University of Toronto School of Continuing Studies. He is the author of fourteen books, including the poetry collections *The Open Room* (1989), *Radio Silence* (1991), and *The Presence* (1999). *The One Story: Literature and the Great Books* was published in 2000.

Leslie Monsour was born in Hollywood, California, but grew up in Mexico City, Chicago, and Panama. She is the author of two chapbooks: *Earth's Beauty, Desire, & Loss*, and *Indelibility*.

Aífe Murray is a poet, mixed media artist, and affiliated scholar with the Institute for Research on Women and Gender at Stanford University. Her visual work, on Dickinson and her servants, has been exhibited in California and the Mead Art Museum, Amherst College. In 1997, in conjunction with the Mead exhibit "Language as Object: Emily Dickinson and Contemporary Art," she led a public tour of the town of Amherst from the perspective of the Dickinson servants.

Marilyn Nelson is the author of five books, including *The Fields of Praise: New and Selected Poems* (1997), a finalist for the 1997 National Book Award; *Magnificat* (1994); *The Homeplace* (1990), also a finalist for the 1991 National Book Award; *Mama's Promises* (1985); and *For the Body* (1978). She has also published two collections of verse for children: *The Cat Walked Through the Casserole and Other Poems for Children* (with Pamela Espeland, 1984) and *Halfdan Rasmussen's Hundreds of Hens and Other Poems for Children* (1982), translated from Danish with Pamela Espeland. Since 1978 she has taught at the University of Connecticut, Storrs, where she is a professor of English.

Peter Nicholson was born in 1950 in Waverly, New South Wales. He was educated at Armidale Teachers' College and Macquarie University. He has published three books, *A Temporary Grace* (1991), *Such Sweet Thunder* (1994), and *A Dwelling Place* (1997). He is currently preparing *New and Selected Poems* for publication in 2001.

Kathleen Norris is the author of several collections of essays, including *Dakota: A Spiritual Geography* and *The Cloister Walk*, as well as the collections of poems *The Middle of the World* and *Little Girls in Church*. She lives and writes in Lemmon, South Dakota.

Joyce Carol Oates is the author of a number of books of poetry including most recently *Tenderness* and *The Time Traveller*. She is professor of humanities at Princeton University. In 1996, she edited *The Essential Emily Dickinson*.

Sharon Olds is the author of six collections of poems, including *The Dead and the Living*, winner of the National Book Critics Circle Award, and most recently, *Blood, Tin, Straw*. She teaches in the graduate creative writing program at New York University and helps run the New York University workshop program at Goldwater Hospital on Roosevelt Island in New York. She was appointed New York State Poet Laureate for 1998–2000.

Alicia Suskin Ostriker's most recent collection of poems is *The Little Space: Poems Selected and New, 1968–1998*. Her other books of poetry include *The Crack in Everything* (1996), which won a National Book Award, and *The Imaginary Lover* (1986). She is also the author of *Dancing at the Devil's Party: Essays on Poetry, Politics and the Erotic*. Her critical works include *The Nakedness of the Fathers: Biblical Visions and Revisions* (1994) and *Stealing the Language: The Emergence of Women's Poetry in America* (1986).

Maureen Owen is the author of eight collections of poems, most recently *American Rush: Selected Poems*. Her collection *AE (Amelia Earhart)* received the Before Columbus American Book Award. Born in Minnesota, raised in California, she currently lives in Connecticut.

Ron Padgett is the founding member of the Teachers and Writers Collaborative in New York City and has taught for more than thirty years in the poetry-in-the-schools programs throughout the country. His is the author of twenty-five collections of poems, translations, and books on education. His *New and Selected Poems* appeared in 1995.

Linda Pastan's tenth book of poems, *Carnival Evening: New and Selected Poems: 1968–1998*, was a finalist for the National Book Award. From 1991 to 1994 she served as Poet Laureate of Maryland.

Andrea Paterson is a writer and lawyer who lives in Washington, D.C. She has previously published poetry and parody and is currently working on a novel.

Molly Peacock is the author of four collections of poems, most recently *Original*

*Love* as well as a memoir, *Paradise, Piece by Piece. How to Read a Poem and Start a Poetry Circle* was published in 1999. She was the founder of the "Poetry in Motion™" program and coeditor of *Poetry in Motion: 100 Poems from the Subways and Buses.* She lives in New York City and London, Ontario.

Robert Peters is the author of numerous collections of poetry and criticism, among them *Poems: Selected & New 1967–1991; The Great American Poetry Bake-Off, 4th Series; Where the Bee Sucks: Workers, Drones and Queens of Contemporary American Poetry;* and *Hunting the Snark: American Poetry at Century's End, Classification and Commentary.* A memoir, *Crunching Gravel: A Wisconsin Boyhood in the Thirties,* was published in 1993. He lives in Huntington Beach, California.

John Reinhard is the author of two poetry collections, *On the Road to Patsy Cline* and *Burning the Prairie.* He earned his MFA from the University of Michigan and teaches in the creative writing program at the University of Alaska-Fairbanks.

Donald Revell is the author of six collections of poetry, most recently *There Are Three* and *Beautiful Shirt.* His translation of Apollinaire's *Alcools* was published in 1995. He is professor of English at the University of Utah.

Adrienne Rich is the author of twenty volumes of poetry, including *Collected Early Poems 1950–1970; Diving into the Wreck,* winner of the National Book Award in 1974; *The Fact of a Doorframe: Poems Selected and New 1950–1984; Dark Fields of the Republic: Poems 1991–1995;* and most recently, *Midnight Salvage: Poems 1995–1998* (1999). Her collections of nonfiction prose include: *Of Woman Born: Motherhood as Experience and Institution* (1976); *On Lies, Secrets, and Silence: Selected Prose, 1966–1978; Blood, Bread, and Poetry: Selected Prose 1979–1986; Women and Honor: Some Notes on Lying* (1990); and *What Is Found There?: Notebooks on Poetry and Politics* (1993).

Larry Rubin has published several books of poetry including, most recently, *Unanswered Calls.* A professor of English, he retired from Georgia Technical College in 1999.

Mary Jo Salter, a former poetry editor of *The New Republic,* is the author of three collections of poetry, most recently *Sunday Skates;* a novel, *A Kiss in Space;* and a children's book, *The Moon Comes Home.* She lives in Massachusetts.

Gary Smith earned his Ph.D. in American Literature from Stanford University. He teaches at DePaul University and is coauthor of a volume of critical essays on Gwendolyn Brooks, *A Life Distilled: Gwendolyn Brooks, Her Poetry and Fiction* and the poetry collections *Songs for My Fathers* and *Psalms for my Mothers.*

Barton Levi St. Armand has taught English and environmental literature in the American Civilization program at Brown University since 1968. In 1984, he published *Emily Dickinson and Her Culture: The Soul's Society.* He is the author of a collection of poems, *Hypogeum: Poems of the Buried Life* and a forthcoming collection of haiku in English.

William Stafford's posthumous collection, *The Way it Is: New and Selected Poems,* was published in 1998. The author of more than fifty books of poetry and prose, Stafford won the National Book Award for Poetry in 1963 for *Traveling Through the Dark*. Stafford taught at Lewis and Clark College in Portland, Oregon, for more than thirty years. He died in 1993.

Lynn Strongin was born in New York City in 1939. She studied composition at the Manhattan School of Music and literature at Hunter College, Stanford University, and the University of New Mexico. She has published a novel, five chapbooks, and two full-length books of poetry, *Countrywoman / Surgeon*, a finalist for the 1979 Elliston Award, and *Bones & Kim*. She lives in Victoria, British Columbia.

Thom Tammaro is Professor of Multidisciplinary Studies and a former director of the New Center for Multidisciplinary Studies at Minnesota State University Moorhead. He is the coeditor of two award-winning anthologies: *Imagining Home: Writing from the Midwest* and *Inheriting the Land: Contemporary Voices from the Midwest*. He is also the author of two collections of poems, *When the Italians Came to My Home Town* and *Minnesota Suite*.

Mark Vinz is professor of English and teaches in the MFA in Creative Writing program at Minnesota State University Moorhead. He is the author of several collections of poetry, including *Late Night Calls* and, most recently, *Affinities* (1999), in collaboration with photographer Wayne Gudmundson.

Theodore Weiss has published fourteen volumes of poetry, the latest being his *Selected Poems*. For over fifty years his wife Renee and he have edited the *Quarterly Review of Literature*. Recently they won a PEN Club Special Lifetime Award for their editing, and Ted received the William / Derwood Prize for his poetry. They are completing a collaborative volume of poems.

Richard Wilbur is the author of more than twenty-five collections of poetry and translations, among them *New and Collected Poems* (1988), winner of the Pulitzer Prize. He also won a Pulitzer Prize and the National Book Award for *Things of This World* (1956). *The Catbird's Song: Prose Pieces* was published in 2000. In 1988 he was appointed U.S. Poet Laureate. He lives in Cummington, Massachusetts.

Diane Williams is the editor and founder of the new literary annual *Noon*. She is the author of *The Stupefaction* and, most recently, *Excitability: Selected Stories*.

Yvor Winters, teacher, poet, and critic, was born in Chicago in 1900 and taught at Stanford University from 1928 to 1966. His *Collected Poems* appeared in 1978 and a revised edition was published in 1980. He died in 1968.

Harold Witt worked as a librarian and freelance writer in Nevada and California and served for many years as a poetry editor at *Blue Unicorn* and *Poet Lore*. His collections of poems include *American Lit*, an autobiographical sequence of sonnets (1994), *Now, Swim* (1974), and *Winesburg by the Sea: Poems*. He died in 1995.

Charles Wright is the author of more than twelve collections of poems, including *Black Zodiac* (1997), winner of the Pulitzer Prize, and *Country Music: Selected Early Poems* (1983), winner of the National Book Award. His collections of nonfiction prose include *Quarter Notes* (1995) and *Halflife* (1988). He teaches in the writing program at the University of Virginia in Charlottesville.

Ray Young Bear was born in Iowa in 1950 and grew up in the Meskwaki Nation of central Iowa. He has been a visiting faculty member at Eastern Washington University, Iowa State University, and the University of Iowa. He is the author of two autobiographical novels, *Remnants of the First Earth* (1998) and *Black Eagle Child: The Face Painting Narratives* (1997), and several collections of poems, including *Winter of the Salamander* and *The Invisible Musician*. With his wife, Stella, and his son, Jesse, he is cofounder of the Black Eagle Child Dance Troupe. Under the Woodland Singers title, they have recorded traditional Meskwaki songs. He lives in Tama, Iowa.

# Permissions

We are grateful to the authors who have given us permission to include previously published work in this anthology. We also thank the authors, editors, and publishers who have given us permission to reprint poems.

Jean Balderston, "'Miss Emily's Maggie' Remembers," from the *Emily Dickinson International Society Bulletin.* Copyright © 1993 by Jean Balderston. Reprinted by permission of the author.

Marvin Bell, "The Mystery of Emily Dickinson," from *Stars Which See, Stars Which Do Not See,* Athenaeum. Copyright © 1977 by Marvin Bell. Reprinted by permission of the author.

John Berryman, "Your Birthday in Wisconsin You Are 140," from *Collected Poems: 1937–1971* by John Berryman. Copyright © 1989 by Kate Donahue Berryman. Reprinted by permission of Farrar, Straus, Giroux, LLC.

Robert Bly, "Visiting Emily Dickinson's Grave with Robert Francis," from *The Man in the Black Coat Turns,* HarperCollins. Copyright © 1999 by Robert Bly. Reprinted by permission of the author.

Marianne Boruch, "For Emily Dickinson," from *Mass Burning,* Oberlin College Press. Copyright © 1993 by Marianne Boruch. Reprinted by permission of the author.

Lucie Brock-Broido, "Queen Recluse," from *The New Republic.* Copyright © 1991 by Lucie Brock-Broido. Reprinted by permission of the author.

Jayne Relaford Brown, "Emily Dickinson Attends a Writing Workshop," from *In The Palm of Your Hand: The Poet's Portable Workshop,* Tilbury House. Copyright © 1995 by Jayne Relaford Brown. Reprinted by permission of the author. Emily Dickinson, "My Life Had Stood a Loaded Gun." Reprinted by the publishers and Trustees of Amherst College from *The Poems of Emily Dickinson,* R. W. Franklin, ed., Cambridge, Mass.: The Belknap Press of Harvard University, copyright © 1998 by the President and Fellows of Harvard College. Copyright © 1951, 1955, 1979 by the President and Fellows of Harvard College.

Andrea Carlisle, "Emily Dickinson's To-Do List," from *I Feel A Little Jumpy Around You: A Book of Her Poems & His Poems Collected in Pairs,* ed. Naomi Shihab Nye and Paul B. Janeczko. Copyright © 1996 by Andrea Carlisle. Reprinted by permission of the author.

Siv Cedering, "Give Me Shoots, You Said." Copyright © 1999 by Siv Cedering. Reprinted by permission of the author.

Amy Clampitt, "Amherst," from *The Collected Poems of Amy Clampitt* by Amy Clampitt. Copyright © 1997 by the Estate of Amy Clampitt. Reprinted by permission of Alfred A. Knopf, Inc.

# Index to Titles